GREAT TALES
FROM
ENGLISH
HISTORY

GREAT TALES
FROM
ENGLISH
HISTORY

*Captain Cook, Samuel Johnson,
Queen Victoria, Charles Darwin,
Edward the Abdicator, and More*

ROBERT LACEY

 LITTLE, BROWN AND COMPANY
New York ∾ Boston ∾ London

Little, Brown and Company
Hachette Book Group USA
1271 Avenue of the Americas, New York, NY 10020
Visit our Web site at www.HachetteBookGroupUSA.com

First published in Great Britain by Little, Brown and Company, 2006
First North American edition, December 2006

We thank Methuen Publishing Ltd. for kind permission to reprint on page 228
the cover illustration by John Reynolds from *1066 and All That* by W. C. Sellar
and R. J. Yeatman; and Souvenir Press Ltd. for permission to quote "The Life
That I Have" from the poetry collection of the same name by Leo Marks.

ISBN 0-316-11459-6 / 978-0-316-11459-2
LCCN 2006931723

10 9 8 7 6 5 4 3 2 1

Q-MART

Printed in the United States of America

FOR BRUNO

CONTENTS

CONTENTS

The Stuarts

James VI of Scotland
James I
1603-25

Henry
d.1612

Elizabeth = Frederick V,
d.1662   Elector Palatine

Charles I
1625-49

Charles II
1660-85

Mary = William II
d.1660 of Orange
        d.1650

Anne (1) = James II = Mary (2) of
Hyde   1685-88   Modena
d.1671   d.1718

Sophia, Electress
of Hanover
d.1714

William III = Mary
1689-1702   1689-94

Anne
1702-14

James Edward
Stuart d.1766
('The Old Pretender')

George I
1714-27

The Hanoverians

Charles Edward
Stuart d.1788
('The Young Pretender')

George II
1727-60

Frederick
Prince of Wales
d.1751

George III
1760-1820

George IV
1820-30

William IV
1830-37

Edward
Duke of Kent
d. 1820

6 other sons
+6 daughters

Victoria
1837-1901

Victoria and Her Descendants

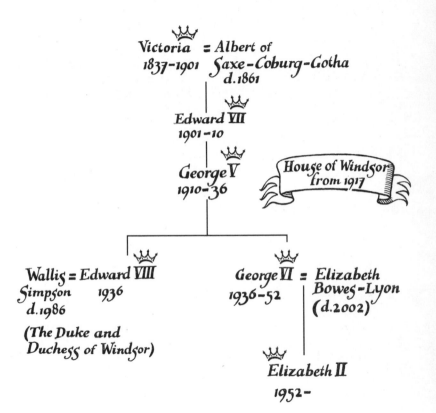

Victoria = Albert of
1837–1901   Saxe-Coburg-Gotha
d.1861

Edward VII
1901–10

George V
1910–36

House of Windsor from 1917

Wallis = Edward VIII
Simpson   1936
d.1986

(The Duke and
Duchess of Windsor)

George VI = Elizabeth
1936–52   Bowes-Lyon
              (d.2002)

Elizabeth II
1952–

GREAT TALES
FROM
ENGLISH
HISTORY

TALE OF A WHALE

LAST WEEK A WHALE SWAM PAST THE BOTTOM of my road. I live about a hundred yards from the Thames, in Pimlico, central London, so when the news came on the radio, I dashed down to the river to take a look.

There were hundreds of people there already, focusing their binoculars and clutching flasks of tea. It was rather a cheery, holiday happening – but also, in some way, an historic moment. Parents had brought their children to witness this event of a lifetime. Peering under the bridges, we could see that gallant volunteers had waded into the water to try to shoo the bewildered creature back downriver. When it became clear she could not do the job herself, they hoisted her on to a rescue barge.

I saw the barge come steaming back downstream, heading for the mouth of the river. It was travelling fast. On the deck we could make out the grey, shiny mass of the whale, surrounded by the volunteers splashing water over her. Could they keep her alive for long enough? we wondered. Could they make it to the open sea?

In the event, our hopes were dashed. The whale died, still on board the barge, in the estuary of the Thames, and the papers next day mourned her passing. One asked its readers for £10,000 to save the animal's bones for the nation, and there were agonised heart-searchings – could more have been done to save 'celebrity big blubber'?

It all made a striking contrast to the year 1240, in the reign of King Henry III, when a whale swam under London Bridge and the citizens pursued it upstream to Mortlake. They harpooned the creature to death – and when, four centuries later, another 'beast of prodigious size' lost its way in the river, it was similarly set upon, to be sliced up and borne away in oil-dripping chunks. The date was 3 June 1658, following 'an extraordinary storm of hail and rain, the season as cold as winter', and this disruption of nature's course was taken to be a significant omen. Oliver Cromwell fell ill that summer, and died three months later.

From old-time slaughter to modern empathy, with some ancient superstition along the way, the history of London's human–whale interaction from 1240 to 2006 would seem to demonstrate that mankind's finer feelings have made progress over the years. What a concentration of human goodwill was beamed towards that whale!

But consider how, in the centuries before people flicked a switch to light their homes, whale oil was a premier source of clean and bright illumination – a precious commodity. Then spare a few minutes, if you can bear it, to survey the superstitious omens on offer in the average modern horoscope column. Add in the tens of thousands of pounds that were spent in January 2006 on helicopters, cameras and whale punditry to turn the lingering death of a tragically disoriented mammal into a round-the-clock source of popular entertainment, and perhaps you will arrive at a different perspective – from level-headed survival to empty-headed sentimentality, perhaps? At least the harpooners of 1240 and 1658 put the poor animal out of its misery with dispatch.

The verdict is yours, dear reader. The job of the historian is to deal objectively with the available facts. But history is in the eye of the beholder *and* also of the historian who, as a human being, has feelings and prejudices of his own. In the two previous paragraphs you have seen the tale of the whale designed and redesigned to offer you two alternative conclusions.

So let me try to be candid about some of my own prejudices. I believe passionately in the power of good storytelling, not only because it is fun, but because it breathes life into the past. It is also through accurate narrative – establishing what happened first and what happened next – that we start to perceive the cause of things, and what influences human beings to act in the noble and cruel ways that they do. I believe that nobility actually secures more effective outcomes than cruelty, though the story of the slave trade in the pages that follow might seem to challenge that. I also believe that ideas matter, that change is possible, that knowledge dispels fear, and that good history both explains and facilitates all those things.

This volume, the third and final part of my 'Great Tales from English History', opens in 1690, and describes what flowed from the momentous agreement of 13 February 1689, the day when England's Parliament concluded its negotiations with Willem van Oranje,* the Dutch prince who had forcibly captured the country four months earlier. As we read at the end of volume 2, this 38-year-old Willem the Conqueror had assembled the largest invasion force ever to land in England and had chased away his father-in-law, the Catholic King James II. Now Willem's blue-coated Dutch soldiers patrolled the streets of London.

The previous morning his wife Mary, daughter of the deposed King, had stepped off a ship from Holland. After changing her clothes and breakfasting at Greenwich, Mary had travelled up the Thames to Westminster to join her husband and add some blood legitimacy to his naked military power.†

Modern history starts here. You might have thought that the execution of Charles I in January 1649 had settled the question as to whether King or Parliament had the final word on how England was to be run. But the bitter divisions of the Civil War, over which more than eighty thousand men had fought and died, had not been resolved by the Cromwell years – and when Charles II was restored in 1660, he had cannily sidestepped attempts to define his powers. The 'Merry Monarch' ruled for a quarter of a century as if his father's head had never been cut off, and from 1685 his brother James nursed a similar confidence that he was

*His title referred to the French town of Orange near Avignon, which had once belonged to his family.
†William had his own, more distant claim to the throne, as the son of Charles I's daughter Mary (see family tree, p. xi)

divinely blessed. It had ended with Willem's invasion and with King James II tearing up the writs summoning Parliament as he stalked off into the night – throwing the Great Seal of England into the Thames for good measure.

Now Parliament determined to get the system right: the King must obey the law; he would have no right to interfere with the country's judges or with the legal system; he must call Parliament regularly and he could levy taxes only with Parliament's consent; the Crown could not interfere with elections, and must also guarantee freedom of speech in debate; no monarch could maintain a standing army in peacetime without Parliament's consent.

All these conditions were read out to Willem van Oranje and his wife Mary on 13 February 1689 as they sat beneath the gloriously painted ceiling of Whitehall's Banqueting Chamber – the last thing that Charles I would have seen as he walked out to be beheaded forty years earlier. When the assembled Lords and Commons heard the couple (both of them grandchildren of the executed King) promise to accept and abide by this 'Declaration of Rights', they offered them the crown. The deal was done. England had the basis of its modern constitutional system of government, and while the future would offer conflicts and turmoil aplenty, with a last Stuart attempt to seize the throne in 1745, there would be no more civil wars.

Stooped and racked with an asthmatic cough, England's third King William was not obvious king material. His only evidence of regality was a head of hair that sprouted so lux-uriantly he did not need to wear a wig. But he had good armies and the right wife. Traditionalists felt Queen Mary

II should now inherit the throne, but William of Orange hadn't led twenty-five thousand soldiers to England in order to end up the consort of his spouse. So Parliament sorted that one out as well. For the first and only time in history, England had joint sovereigns. 'WilliamanMary', as *1066 and All That* would later describe them, were crowned together on 11 April 1689.

It all went to show how the people's elected representatives, meeting with the peers, judges and bishops in the House of Lords, could arrange things in England more or less however they wanted, and so it has proved ever since. From 1690 onwards Parliament would meet every single year – theoretically at the summons of the sovereign, but in reality on the basis of its own hard-won power and authority.

But we should not think of England at this date as a modern parliamentary 'democracy'. Women had no vote at all, and would not get it for another two hundred and thirty years. Elections were decided by the votes of less than 25 per cent of the country's adult males – most of them at the richer, land- and property-owning end of the social scale. There was no secret ballot.

Yet in 1690 there was no country on earth that could match the degree of popular representation that England enjoyed, and this was reflected in a grudging acceptance of different religious points of view. Roman Catholics were marginalised, Jews were often envied and sneered at, while 'Mahometans' were bizarre strangers from beyond the fringe of the civilised world. But the suspicious and previously warring factions of the Protestant faith had negotiated a coexistence that was the envy of visiting foreigners. England's liberty of worship, declared the French philosopher Voltaire, who fled from Paris to London in 1726 to escape the intolerance of an absolute monarchy, was the secret of the country's great achievements.

We shall read of these achievements in the pages that follow – of how English and Scottish enterprise helped manufacture 'Great Britain' with its massive military might and its much celebrated dominion of the seas. In many respects this third and final volume leaves England behind, to recount Great Tales of *British* History, in which the English, Irish, Scots and Welsh, while remaining healthily fractious, collaborate as never before – not least in the creation of the world-wide British Empire. This profitable adventure, which involved considerable loss of life, was built on the world's first ever 'Industrial Revolution', on countless individual tales of success and suffering – and, yes, on the slave trade, that profoundly shaming sin. The political context for all these complex developments was provided by the deal that Willem the Dutchman struck with Parliament on 13 February 1689.

Later that year King William III would cross to Ireland to fight the campaign that culminated in the Battle of the Boyne, ensuring that his deal beneath the painted ceiling – soon to be celebrated as the 'Glorious Revolution' – would have a chance to bear fruit. But let us start with the philosopher who put the inspiring idea of toleration into words.

JOHN LOCKE AND TOLERATION

1690

SNOW FELL HEAVILY IN HOLLAND IN THE winter of 1683, and one of the victims of the cold was a lioness that died in the Amsterdam zoo. As Dutch academics gathered for the rare opportunity to dissect the corpse of an exotic beast, they were joined by an English doctor and philosopher, John Locke. Locke had recently arrived in Amsterdam and when he struck up a conversation with Philip van Limborch, a local professor of theology, the exchange between the two men soon extended far beyond the autopsy. They both had an interest, they discovered, in religious toleration – it was a burning issue of the moment – and van Limborch encouraged Locke to set his thoughts down on paper.

Locke, fifty-one, was a political exile in Holland. A small-time lawyer's son from the Somerset village of Wrington, he had been a teenager during the Civil War, then studied at Oxford University in the years following the death of Charles I. As religious sects quarrelled and the army made and unmade parliaments, the visionary chaos of Cromwell's England started pushing Locke to consider that there must be some more stable and rational way of government. The essence of civil society, he came to feel, should be a fair working contract between the governor and the governed, and this had inclined him to welcome Charles II's return at the invitation of Parliament in 1660.

But the restored King had proved, for all his charm, to be an absolutist like his father. Locke drifted into the Whig, or anti-royal camp, becoming a friend and medical adviser to Anthony Ashley Cooper, the Earl of Shaftesbury, who led the Whig attempt to exclude the future James II from the succession. When Charles defeated the third Exclusion Bill in 1681 and determined to rule without Parliament, Shaftesbury fled for his life to the Netherlands, dying there in 1683. Later that year Locke decided that he too would be safer in the Netherlands, and so found himself, soon after his arrival, in the crowd that gathered around the lioness on the dissecting table.

Shadowed by Stuart agents and hiding under a variety of aliases, Locke was working on the philosophical text for which he would become most famous, *An Essay on Human Understanding*. 'The highest perfection of intellectual nature,' he wrote, 'lies in a careful and constant pursuit of true and solid happiness.'

Looking for happiness in this life might strike many today as the most obvious of goals to pursue, but it was heresy in an age when most people assumed they would only encounter and fully experience their God after they had died. Locke's suggestion that earthly life was something to be enjoyed here and now jarred on many of his contemporaries as 'atheistic'.

In fact, the philosopher was a devout Christian, and in the autumn of 1685 he was appalled by Louis XIV's sudden revocation of the freedom of worship that France's Protestants, the Huguenots, had enjoyed since 1598 under the Edict of Nantes. As Huguenot refugees fled persecution – England alone welcomed fifty thousand – Locke took up his Dutch friend van Limborch's suggestion and sat down to compose *Epistola de tolerantia, A Letter concerning Toleration.* Spiritual belief, Locke argued, was no business of the state, which should confine itself to the 'civil interests' that he defined as 'life, liberty, health and indolency [freedom from pain] of body, and the possession of outward things such as money, land, houses, furniture and the like'.

A century later Thomas Jefferson would combine these words with the key phrase from Locke's *Essay on Human Understanding* to produce his stirring battle cry for 'Life, Liberty and the Pursuit of Happiness'. The US Declaration of Independence would echo round the world.

In his own lifetime, however, Locke felt it safer to keep a low profile. Although he came back to England on 12 February 1689 on the same ship as Princess Mary – who, next day, would strike the deal with Parliament that made her husband and herself joint sovereigns – Locke found it prudent to keep some of his crucial essays anonymous. There was no author's name on *A Letter concerning Toleration*: the title page carried scrambled letters that were code for 'Locke' and 'Limborch', to whom the work was dedicated. Only Locke and the Dutchman knew the code, and Locke acknowledged his authorship of the *Letter* and other works only in a codicil to his will signed the month before his death in October 1704.

By then, people were coming to see that Locke had put into words the essential values of the Glorious Revolution – and particularly in his *Two Treatises on Civil Government* that he published anonymously in 1690. Governments, he wrote, may not 'levy taxes on the people' without 'the consent . . . of their representatives'. No government, he argued, could be considered legitimate unless grounded in the consent of the people – and any ruler who attempted to exercise an arbitrary power 'is to be esteemed the Common enemy and Pest of mankind and is to be treated accordingly'.

Nowadays John Locke is thought of almost exclusively in terms of his political philosophy. He is studied at universities as the apostle of modern Western liberal democracy, as Marx was the apostle of Communism. But in his own lifetime he was a hands-on man of many talents – throwing himself into the vortex of thought and experiment that came to be known as the Enlightenment. Elected a member of the Royal Society, he served on a 'committee of experiments', and when his patron Lord Shaftesbury fell ill, he supervised the risky operation that drained an abscess on his liver. Above all, he spoke up for toleration, and was delighted when one of the first statutes of William and Mary's reign was an act that allowed Dissenters (though not Catholics) to worship in their own licensed meeting-houses.

'Toleration has now at last been established by law in our country,' he wrote triumphantly to his lioness autopsy friend, van Limborch. 'Not perhaps so wide in scope as might be wished for by you . . . Still, it is something to have progressed so far.'

'REMEMBER THE BOYNE!' – THE
BIRTH OF THE ORANGEMEN

1690

AT THE BEGINNING OF JULY 1690, KING
William III and his officers sat down for a picnic on the
north bank of the River Boyne, thirty miles north of Dublin.
On the other bank were massed the more numerous forces of
James II, who, having fled from London the previous year,
was now trying to recapture his kingdom with the help of his
loyal Catholic subjects in Ireland and a contingent of crack
French troops. The French King Louis XIV was backing
James as part of his campaign for French and Catholic dom-
ination of Europe.

It was a momentous confrontation – the last between two
rival kings of Britain. Either man could lose everything, and

William nearly did when a stray shot from the southern bank came sailing across the river and smacked into his shoulder, sending him tumbling to the ground. The Jacobites (so named from the Latin for James – *Jacobus*) could not believe their luck. With one stray shot, it seemed, they had reversed the ousting of their Catholic champion the previous year.

But within hours William, calm as ever, was riding among his troops, with his arm in a sling – a token of God's providence and also of his cool Dutch courage. That night he showed his Dutch cunning as well. He dispatched a section of his troops west along the river to the ford of Rosnaree, making enough noise to persuade the Jacobite scouts and sentries that most of his army was on the move.

James responded by breaking camp and marching for Rosnaree with a major contingent to foil this flanking attack. But when the sun rose the next morning, the Jacobite troops that he had left by the Boyne peered through the river mists to see, with horror, that most of William's army was still in place. From having outnumbered their enemy, it was they who were now outnumbered – and one of the mysteries of that day is why the deposed King, when he reached Rosnaree and discovered he had fallen for a ruse, did not come marching back post-haste. James was strangely invisible on this day that would decide his – and Britain's – destiny. The little figure of William with his bandaged arm, by contrast, was much in evidence as his men forded the river and fought their way uphill to eventual victory.

By the end of the following day William was riding into Dublin in triumph – while James, for the third and last time in his career, was escaping from the British Isles as a fugitive.

'I do now resolve,' he declared with resignation, 'to shift for myself.'

William was generous in victory. He allowed some eleven thousand Jacobite soldiers to go freely to France, where they became 'the Wild Geese' – a foreign legion of devil-may-care mercenaries who fought for the Catholic cause in the royal armies of Europe. William also promised Ireland's Catholics 'such privileges in the exercise of their religion . . . as they had enjoyed in the days of Charles II'.

But Ireland's victorious Protestants did not share their new King's spirit of tolerance. It was not easy to expunge the religiously entwined hatreds between settler and native that went back, via Oliver Cromwell's atrocities of the 1650s, to the original colonisation by the Normans. In the months before the Boyne, during the brief period when James II controlled the island, the Catholics had been merciless. Taking their revenge for centuries of subjection, they had dispossessed Protestants of their land, pushing them back to their northern strongholds in Ulster, and particularly to the town of Derry, where the local apprentice boys rationed the available oatmeal and horsemeat in a desperate siege that lasted 105 days before the army of 'King Billy' relieved them.

Now the Protestants in turn took their revenge. In 1691 Catholics were excluded from Ireland's Parliament and, the next year, from serving in the army; Protestants could carry firearms, but Catholics could not. In subsequent years Catholics were excluded from public office and prevented from building up large estates – all this making brutally clear that Ireland was, in effect, a colony and its Catholics second-class citizens. In 1720 the Declaratory Act laid down that while London had the right to veto acts passed by the Irish Parliament, Ireland must accept all legislation that Westminster might send the other way.

The hatreds have lingered poisonously into the present. At the Boyne, William of Orange's troops wore orange sashes, and to this day the Apprentice Boys and the bowler-hatted men of the Orange Order, now mainly concentrated in the counties of Northern Ireland, march proudly every July to commemorate the victory of King Billy. The annual 'marching season' seldom fails to bring Ireland's sectarian bigotry to the boil, with bitterness – and, not infrequently, bloodshed.

'Remember the Boyne!' The rest of the British Isles has come to see the factious anniversary of this battle as a peculiarly Irish obsession. In fact, the victory deserves wider celebration, since it guaranteed England and Scotland the benefits of the 'Glorious Revolution' – restraint, equality, and respect for the law. These were the forward-looking principles that the real King Billy made possible in his unexciting but effective way, and it seems unfair that the Orange King should have become the symbol for the perversely backward-looking values that still bedevil Northern Ireland.

'1690?' runs a message on the wall of one Catholic ghetto. 'Let's have a replay!'

BRITANNIA RULES THE WAVES –
THE TRIANGULAR TRADE

1693

ON 18 NOVEMBER 1693 CAPTAIN THOMAS Phillips was sailing his ship the *Hannibal* along the west coast of Africa, when he made a curious discovery. One of the young black soldiers on board, by the name of John Brown, was not a man but a woman. Her true sex had been discovered when she fell ill and the ship's surgeon had ordered a 'glister'. Administering this enema, or rectal poultice, the surgeon's assistant 'was surpriz'd to find more sally-ports than he expected'.

Captain Phillips immediately arranged separate quarters for the young woman, and had the ship's tailor make up for her some female clothing. She had been living on the all-male ship for several months – she had fooled the recruiters of the Royal Africa Company and had enlisted in London to serve in one of their forts along the coast of 'Guinea', as West Africa was known. Was she one of the 'blackamoor' community that had existed in London for more than a century? The blackamoors were descendants, for the most part, of imported black African slaves – and this enterprising twenty-year-old probably disguised herself as a soldier to get back 'home' to Guinea. But what was her real name, and what had inspired her to hide under the identity of 'John Brown'?

History, sadly, gives us no answers to these questions, for having repaid Captain Phillips for his kindness by washing his linen, 'John Brown' disembarked with the other, truly male soldiers at Cape Coast Castle (in modern Ghana), vanishing from the pages of the captain's log and of any other surviving record. Yet her intriguing adventure does open the door on to the bizarre and scandalous commerce that would help make thousands of Englishmen very rich in the next century or so – the transatlantic slave trade, also known as the triangular trade.

The *Hannibal* had been sailing south on the first leg of this triangle when Captain Phillips discovered 'John Brown'. By this date English slave-traders had been travelling down to Guinea for more than thirty years with cargoes of cloth, guns, brass, knives, beads, mirrors, cooking pots, beer, cider, brandy and the occasional horse, which they would use to purchase slaves – men, women and children – captured by local traders and warrior chiefs. The soldiers on board the *Hannibal* were on their way to garrison the little beachside castles with which the Royal Africa Company, founded by Charles II, protected the slavers from attack.

The second leg of the triangle carried the slaves westwards across the Atlantic to be sold to the plantation owners in England's colonies in North America and the Caribbean – the *Hannibal* was heading for the sugar plantations on the island of Barbados. This so-called Middle Passage was marked by conditions of the most appalling barbarity, starting with the branding of each slave on the breast or shoulder with a hot iron – 'the place before being anointed with a little palm oil which caused but little pain', according to Captain Phillips, 'the mark [usually the first letter of the ship's name] being usually well in four or five days, appearing very plain and white'.

Shackled and stacked like so many books on a shelf, the captive Africans endured unspeakable squalor in the dark and fetid holds of the slave ships. One in eight died on the voyage. Twice a day they were taken up on deck, chained in pairs, for fresh air, a pint of water and two pints of soup. But infected by the urine and excrement in which they lay, many succumbed to 'the flux' – vomiting and diarrhoea. Other vessels would try to keep upwind of the slave ships, which were notorious for their noxious stink.

Unloaded for sale on the other side of the Atlantic, the human cargoes were poked and prodded, their jaws clamped open for teeth inspection, their private parts fondled, on occasions, and exposed to inspection of a still more demeaning sort. 'Do you not buy them and use them merely as you do horses to labour for your commodity?' protested Richard Baxter, the Puritan preacher. 'How cursed a crime it is to equal men to beasts.'

But few others saw it that way. African slaves provided cheap, sturdy labour – and profits. John Locke was an investor in the Royal Africa Company, along with most of the English court and the political elite. England was developing a profitable sweet tooth, along with a free-spending taste for other addictive substances – coffee, tobacco and rum (distilled from cane sugar). Only muscular young men who were acclimatised to working in a tropical climate could handle the back-breaking labour of the plantations that produced sugar, tobacco and also cotton.

These were the cargoes that now filled the slave ships – sluiced down and considerably cleaner than they had been on the Middle Passage – as they sailed home on the third and final leg of their triangular voyage that had lasted between a year and eighteen months. In the 1690s London provided both the start and the finish for most of these lucrative ventures, but Bristol would take over in the 1730s with roughly forty trips a year, and Liverpool took over after that. By the end of the eighteenth century this one-time fishing village at the mouth of the Mersey was a prosperous metropolis from whose grand stone quays and warehouses a hundred slave ships were sailing every year.

The profits of the triangular trade helped fuel the spectacular economic take-off that the whole of England – and later Scotland – would enjoy in the eighteenth century, along with the prosperous growth of Britain's overseas Empire and the control of the seas celebrated in 'Rule

Britannia', the hit song of 1740: 'Britons never, never, never shall be slaves.'

But that would not prevent Britons from buying and selling them.

JETHRO TULL'S 'DRILL' AND THE
MINER'S FRIEND

1701

LIKE MANY AN INNOVATOR, JETHRO TULL
was something of a crank. In 1701 he got annoyed when
the labourers on his Oxfordshire farm refused to follow his
instructions for planting sainfoin, a clover-like fodder plant
that took its name from the French – literally, 'wholesome
hay'. Educated at Oxford University and trained as a barrister, Jethro reckoned he had the wit, as he later put it, to
'contrive an engine to plant St Foin more faithfully than
[paid] hands would do'. Machines, unlike 'hands', did not
answer back. '[So] I examined and compared all the mechanical ideas that ever had entered my imagination.'

This gentleman farmer found his inspiration in the soundboard of a musical instrument – an organ, whose grooves and holes suggested to him a way that sainfoin seeds could be channelled into the earth at a controlled rate. To the rear of this device Jethro added the spikes of a harrow that would rake soil over the seed, and he named his new machine a 'drill' – 'because,' he explained, 'when farmers used to sow their beans and peas into channels or furrows by hand, they called that action drilling'.

Jethro Tull was ahead of his time. It would be a century and a half before factory-made mechanical seed drills were a common sight on English farms. Some of Jethro's theories actually held back farming progress – he opposed the use of manure, for example, on the grounds that it encouraged the spread of weeds. But *Horse-Hoeing Husbandry*, the book that he wrote to publicise his inventions, encouraged England's farmers to think in scientific and mechanical terms, and this made an important contribution to the movement that historians would later call the 'Agricultural Revolution'.

The efficient production of low-priced food meant that the typical eighteenth-century English family did not have to spend nearly everything it earned on bread, as was the case in France before 1789. They had spare money for shopping. Economists have identified this surplus purchasing power as one of the factors contributing to Britain's so-called *Industrial Revolution*, with people spending their spare cash on the consumer goods that started to emerge from the growing number of '[manu]factories'.

Many of these new factories would come to depend on the efficiencies made possible by harnessing the power of steam, and this breakthrough was first announced in the year after Jethro invented his drill.

The year 1702 saw the publication in London of *The Miner's Friend – or a Description of an Engine to raise Water by Fire* by Thomas Savery, a Devonshire naval engineer who devised a means of powering ships by mechanical paddles. The navy turned down Savery's suggestion for a paddle-boat, but he had more luck with his 'Miner's Friend', a machine he devised to improve the efficiency and safety of Cornwall's tin mines. A coal-fired boiler heated water to produce steam. When cooled, the steam created a vacuum that drew up water from the mineshaft as a primitive pump.

This pumping action was improved a few years later by another Devonshire inventor, Thomas Newcomen, who collaborated with Savery and added a piston to his process. Newcomen's piston dramatically increased the volume of water that could be brought to the surface, and by the time of his death in 1729 more than a hundred such steam pumps were working in British tin and coal mines. Standing at the head of the pit shaft, Newcomen's heavy beam, rocking to and fro to the sighing of the steam and the creaking of the piston, was the technological marvel of the age.

But Newcomen did not die a wealthy man – the canny Savery had taken out a patent extending to 1733, which covered all engines that 'raised Water by Fire'. Like Jethro Tull, Newcomen furthered technological progress, but scarcely profited from it.

MARLBOROUGH CATCHES THE FRENCH SLEEPING AT THE VILLAGE OF THE BLIND

1704

A S DAWN ROSE ON 13 AUGUST 1704 OVER the village of Blindheim in southern Germany, a French officer was horrified to wake and see the red and white uniforms of an English army advancing towards him in full battle array. Riding hell for leather back into the French camp, he found his troops in their tents fast asleep – they had all thought the English were miles away. The battle that followed at Blindheim (literally, 'the home of the blind') would rank as England's greatest military triumph since Agincourt, and would make the reputation of the general who accomplished it – John Churchill, Duke of Marlborough.

Churchill specialised in dawn surprises. Early on 24 November 1688 he had led four hundred officers and men out of the camp of King James II on Salisbury Plain to join the invading army of William of Orange – it was the key defection in the Dutchman's bloodless takeover. Rewarded with the earldom of Marlborough, Churchill would build a spectacular military career based on imagination, administrative ability and a willingness to lead from the front.

But Churchill's bravery was matched by his arrogance, vanity and deviousness – for many years he maintained a secret correspondence with the exiled James II and in 1694 even betrayed the battle plans for a British naval attack on the French port of Brest. Churchill also played domestic politics with the help of his equally ambitious wife Sarah, who used her position as best friend and confidante of Queen Mary's younger sister Anne to intrigue at court on her husband's behalf.

Following the death of Mary in 1694 and then William in 1702, Anne became Queen in her own right, and the Churchills, John and Sarah, made full use of the wealth and influence that went with being the power-couple behind the throne. In 1702 Sarah controlled the three main jobs in the new Queen's household – she was groom of the stole, mistress of the robes and keeper of the privy purse – while John, now Knight of the Garter, was 'Captain-General of her Majesty's land forces and Commander-in-Chief of forces to be employed in Holland in conjunction with troops of the allies'.

England was then at war with France, the so-called War of the Spanish Succession that followed the death of the mad and childless Carlos II of Spain. The conflict had been sparked in 1701 when Louis XIV backed his grandson Philip's claim to the entire Spanish Empire that included large areas of Italy. Not content with that, he had recognised James II's son, James Francis Edward Stuart (the child believed by Protestants to have been smuggled into the royal birthing bed in a warming pan), as 'King James III' of England. To resist the French King's bid for a 'universal monarchy', England, the Netherlands and Austria had banded together in a 'Grand Alliance' – and the Earl of Marlborough was given command of the English and Dutch forces.

Marlborough's problem was that Holland viewed its army primarily as a defence force. The Dutch did not want their soldiers deployed too far from home. So Marlborough did not tell his allies the full story as he headed south towards the River Mosel. Swinging eastwards, he made a series of forced marches, travelling from 3 to 9 a.m. in the morning in order to avoid the summer heat and the French spies. At every halt, masterly planning had fresh horses, food and clothing awaiting his troops – in Heidelberg there was a new pair of boots for every soldier. Meeting up with Prince Eugene, the Austrian commander, Marlborough went to view the enemy encampment at Blindheim from the top of a church tower on 12 August, and the two men agreed to make a surprise attack next day.

The allies were outnumbered by the Franco-Bavarian forces but they had surprise on their side, plus a disciplined aggression which Marlborough's training had instilled into the formerly despised English soldiery. 'The rapidity of their movements together with their loud yells, were truly alarming,' recalled one French officer.

By the end of the day, the Franco-Bavarian army had suffered some 20,000 killed and wounded, compared to 12,000 on the allied side. As dusk fell, Marlborough scribbled a message to his wife on the back of a tavern bill: 'I have not time to say more but to beg you will give my duty to the Queen and let her know her army has had a glorious victory.'

When the message reached London eight days later the capital went wild. It was a memorable victory, overturning the country's reputation as an offshore also-ran. A service of thanksgiving was held in the newly built St Paul's Cathedral, printers turned out copies of the tavern-bill note, and Parliament voted Marlborough a dukedom and a huge sum of money. The Queen gave her friend's husband land from the old royal estate at Woodstock near Oxford, and on it the new Duke and Duchess of Marlborough would erect a magnificent palace named after the popular English rendering of Blindheim – Blenheim.

In the years that followed, Marlborough won victories at Ramillies (1706), Oudenarde (1708) and Malplaquet (1709). But the last of these cost thirty thousand allied lives – it was 'a very murdring battel', as Marlborough himself confessed, and English opinion began to turn against the war. The revelation that the great man had enriched himself from the sale of bread to his armies led to charges of embezzlement, and on New Year's Eve 1711 he was sacked by his wife's former best friend, Queen Anne.

Disabled by strokes, John Churchill died in 1722, pitifully broken in body and mind. But his palace at Blenheim remains a splendid memorial to a great general and an historic victory, and was to be the birthplace a century and a half later of another battling Churchill – Winston. Britain's inspirational leader in the Second World War was a direct descendant of the first Duke of Marlborough.

UNION JACK

1707

IN THE SPRING OF 1702 A SHORT-SIGHTED, burrowing mammal became the hero of the Jacobite supporters of the old Catholic Stuart line. William III died from his injuries after his horse stumbled on a molehill in the park at Hampton Court, and the Jacobites thereupon raised their glasses to toast 'the little gentleman in black velvet'.

William had died childless, and Protestants worried at the similar lack of issue in his sister-in-law and successor, Queen Anne. In the seventeen years following her marriage in 1683 to her cousin Prince George of Denmark, Anne had endured no less than nineteen pregnancies that ended in five infant deaths, some thirteen miscarriages and just one

healthy son who died at the age of eleven. This tragic succession of gynaecological failures left Anne an invalid for the
rest of her life and presented Protestant England with a
dilemma – after Anne, the next fifty-seven Stuarts in line to
the throne were all Catholics.

Parliament's solution was the Act of Settlement of 1701.
All fifty-seven Catholics were eliminated from the succes-
sion, which was handed to no. 58, the Protestant Sophia,
Electress of Hanover, a descendant of James I's daughter
Elizabeth (see family tree, p. x).

But Westminster failed to consult Scotland in arriving at
this drastic solution, apparently assuming that the 'northern
kingdom' would meekly go along with whatever monarch
England chose for itself. The Scots were outraged. 'All our
affairs since the union of the crowns have been managed by
the advice of English ministers,' complained one member of
the Scottish Parliament, referring to 1603 when James VI of
Scotland became James I of England. 'We have from that
time appeared . . . more like a conquered province than a
free independent people.'

To reclaim Scotland's independence, its Parliament in
Edinburgh passed an Act of Security asserting that, after
Anne's death, Scotland would choose a Protestant Stuart of
its own – who might not be a Hanoverian. Westminster's
retort was the so-called Alien Act of March 1705. This
threatened that unless Scotland adopted the Hanoverian
succession by December, any Scot who found himself in
England would be treated as an alien, and that Scottish
imports of coal, cattle and linen would be banned.

'Never two Nations that had so much Affinity in

Circumstances,' commented Daniel Defoe, 'have had such Inveteracy and Aversion to one another in their blood.'

Like a long-married couple wrangling, both sides made their points with feeling, but then decided to compromise. In April 1706 two teams of commissioners met in London to negotiate a union between the kingdoms, and they arrived at twenty-five articles of agreement with remarkable speed. Scotland and England would be separate no more: they would become a new single Kingdom of Great Britain with the same Hanoverian on the throne; a single Parliament in Westminster would be expanded to include forty-five Scottish MPs and sixteen Scottish peers; the whole of Great Britain would become a single free-trade zone using the English pound and English weights and measures; but Scotland would keep its own legal system, universities, local town charters and, above all, its own separate Presbyterian Church, the Kirk. All those distinct Scottish entities survive to this day – with the recent addition, in 1997, of a revived Scottish Parliament.

The very first article of the Act of Union, passed early in 1707, described the flag of this new United Kingdom – a combination of Scotland's diagonal white cross of St Andrew on a blue ground with the upright red cross of St George on white (Wales being considered part of England). In fact, Anglo-Scottish ships had been flying this design for more than a century as a small ensign on the bowsprit. Sailors knew it as the 'jack flag', but now it got a new nickname – the Union Jack.

MADE IN GERMANY

1714

IN SEPTEMBER 1714 KING GEORGE I ARRIVED in London in a cavalcade of 260 horse-drawn coaches that took three hours to pass by. In the coaches were more than ninety of his German ministers and courtiers, his two German mistresses – one inordinately fat and the other contrastingly thin – and his much favoured Turkish grooms and body-servants, captured at the siege of Vienna in 1683. None of these companions spoke more than a few words of English, and nor did the King himself. Having passed most of his fifty-four years in the small north German state of Hanover, Georg Ludwig had to converse with his English ministers in a mixture of French and schoolroom Latin.

The family tree on p. x shows the complicated blood route by which Georg Ludwig of Hanover's descent from James I entitled him to become King George I of Great Britain, but his principal qualification was his Protestant faith. 'A Protestant country can never have stable times under a popish Prince,' declared Bishop Richard Willis in 1715, 'any more than a flock of sheep can have quiet when a wolf is their shepherd.'

Understanding this, England's Protestant elite – the gentry, merchants and nobility – flocked to greet the King in the Painted Hall at Greenwich. But the ordinary people felt resentment. On George's coronation day the following month, 'strange tumults and disorders' were reported in Bristol, Norwich, Birmingham and some thirty other towns in the south. In the subsequent months, disturbances became so commonplace in London, the Midlands and along the Welsh border that in July 1715 Parliament passed the Riot Act. This gave the authorities the power to 'read the riot act' to any gathering of twelve people or more: if they refused to disperse within an hour, they could be hanged.

That autumn, 'the Pretender', the tall and thin, white-faced James Francis Edward Stuart, son of James II, landed in Scotland in a bid to reclaim his throne. But though loyalists might secretly toast 'the King over the water', few were prepared to risk their lives. Only a few diehard Roman Catholics rallied to the small Jacobite army as it marched south. If German George was uninspiring, the fastidious, French-educated James III had even less charisma. His troops surrendered at Preston in November 1715, while James himself escaped to Scotland and thence to France.

So the English had to work up some enthusiasm for their short, pop-eyed German monarch, who demonstrated his enthusiasm for them by going off to Hanover every summer and staying there for as long as he could. When George was in London he spent as much time as possible with his fellow Germans, particularly his two mistresses, whom he visited on alternate nights, fat and thin, listening to music, playing cards and amusing himself with such pastimes as cutting out paper silhouettes. His problems with the language discouraged him from getting too involved in England's politics – and that suited England's politicians just fine.

SOUTH SEA BUBBLE

1720

THE WHEELER-DEALERS OF EIGHTEENTH-
century London loved to gather in the city's busy coffee
houses. 'There was a rabble going hither and thither,' wrote
one visitor, 'reminding me of a swarm of rats in a ruinous
cheese store. Some came, others went; some were scrib-
bling, others were talking . . . The whole place stank of
tobacco.'

If the focus of the modern coffee bar is the hissing
espresso machine, in Stuart and Georgian times it was the
row of tall, black coffee pots warming in the open hearth.
Many of London's coffee houses clustered around the Royal
Exchange in the heart of the City between Cornhill and

Threadneedle Street, and when the senior merchants of the Exchange called for quiet and expelled the jabbering stock-jobbers at the end of the seventeenth century, these forerunners of the modern stockbroker shifted their trading to the coffee hearths. For more than seventy years (until 1773), London's stock exchange gesticulated and shouted its business in the coffee houses of Exchange Alley, notably at Jonathan's and Garraway's.

Share-dealing in England went back over a century to the joint-stock companies set up to fund the Tudor voyages of discovery – with foreign exchange dealers, ship insurers and old-fashioned moneylenders all contributing to the profitable bustle of City life. This had taken on a new dimension in 1694 with the founding of the Bank of England, which borrowed from the general public at interest rates ranging from 8 or 9 to as much as 14 per cent in order to lend money to the government. Investors had rushed forward. In its first two weeks of business, the new Bank attracted some twelve hundred of them, including the King and Queen.

In 1711 the South Sea Company was founded as a rival investment opportunity to the Bank, with an exotic twist. The company was busy securing a monopoly of the Spanish slave trade and a share in other trading ventures in the tropics. Soaking up the money of investors great and small, the new institution, ever more ambitious, negotiated with the government to take over part of the National Debt. But this involved bribing ministers and courtiers, including the King's mistresses, with South Sea stock. And, to keep the price up, the company's promoters started making unrealistic promises, offering dividends they could not deliver. 'The town is quite mad about the South Sea,' wrote one observer in March 1720. 'One can hear nothing else talked of.'

By April, South Sea stock had risen from around 130 per cent to over 300, and speculation grew fiercer. 'Surprizing Scene in [Ex]Change Alley,' ran a report on 2 June. 'S. Sea in the morning above 900.'

Aristocrats, fashionable ladies and footmen all joined in the rush to stake their fortunes on South Sea stock. 'Everyone thirsts for more,' came one word of warning at the end of June as shares peaked at over 1000, 'and all this founded upon the machine of paper credit supported only by the imagination'.

Within the bubble grew smaller bubbles – a company to import walnut trees from Virginia, a project to improve the Greenland fisheries – and even 'a company for carrying on an undertaking of great advantage but nobody to know what it is'.

As canny investors realised the folly of the general hysteria and cashed in their shares, the value of South Sea stock began to fall. The bubble was pricked. By September 1720 it was down to 130, and hundreds of thousands of people who had sold land and property to buy near the peak were ruined. Bankruptcy listings in the *London Gazette* reached an all-time high. Suicides were reported, and panic was widespread. As the company directors fled the country, the King signed warrants for their arrest.

At the time, the monstrous bubble produced a shocking and unheard-of train of events. But today we are familiar with the sequence of boom and bust, insider trading, corruption and, finally, the show trials and the verdicts meted out to those with inky fingers. They are the all too familiar ingredients of the modern big-city scam.

BRITAIN'S FIRST
PRIME MINISTER

1721–42

TOWARDS THE END OF AUGUST 1720 ROBERT Walpole MP fancied dipping his toes once again in the profitable waters of the South Sea Company. Four months earlier the hard-drinking and rotund Norfolk politician, who had recently been appointed Paymaster General of the forces, had sold much of his stock at 300 per cent, and had pocketed a tidy profit. Now he sent off a hefty bid for more, greedily eyeing a price that was rising beyond the 1000 mark and seemed to promise him even more riches ...

Luckily for Walpole, there was a delay in the mail and he never spent his money, thereby avoiding financial ruin and earning a reputation for prudence that he did nothing to dispel. The portly Paymaster General actually took on the job of sorting out the mess left by the South Sea Bubble, punishing the most obvious scapegoats but discreetly turning a blind eye to those – like the King and some of his favourite ministers – whose dealings had not been above reproach. In August 1721, Robert Walpole's act 'to restore the publick Credit' was passed by Parliament, and he gained a national pre-eminence that he would enjoy for two decades.

Aged forty-five in 1721, Walpole was the knowing and worldly master of Britain's evolving system of constitutional government. He was, as he said himself, 'no saint, no Spartan, no reformer'. In 1711 he had spent six months in the Tower and been briefly expelled from Parliament for embezzling government money. Politically he was a Whig, a successor of those who had opposed the absolutism of James II and had fought for parliamentary supremacy over the Crown, ushering in the Hanoverians. Not surprisingly George I favoured the Whigs over their Tory opponents, with their lingering allegiance to the Jacobite cause.

Walpole grasped the essence of the new consensus. The monarch might head the government, but the country was run by his ministers, whose authority depended upon Parliament and the House of Commons in particular. 'So great was Walpole's love of the Commons,' wrote the Earl of Chesterfield, 'that when going to face the House, he dressed as carefully as a lover going to see a mistress.'

When Walpole's stature reached the point at which most politicians claimed a peerage and moved up to the House of Lords, he chose to stay in the Commons – the chamber that mattered when it came to government revenue. There he remained for more than twenty years, exercising his power as the monarch's principal, or 'prime', minister – though Walpole himself eschewed the title, preferring to be known as First Lord of the Treasury. This is the official title borne by prime ministers to this day – you will not find the words 'Prime Minister' inscribed on any formal government list.

A genial and relaxed speaker, Walpole unashamedly used patronage to massage his majority in the Commons, handing out government jobs to create an army of dependable place-men – 'all men have their price' was another of his favourite sayings. He made a point of dining privately with every new Whig MP, and he was equally assiduous with his other font of power, the Crown. When George II succeeded his father in 1727, Walpole worked hard to secure the new King a massively generous Civil List, the parliamentary grant first established for William and Mary to cover not only the expenses of the sovereign, their family, household, parks and palaces, but also the salaries and pensions of ministers, judges and other public officials – the civil government, in fact.

Having secured £800,000 for the King, Walpole raised a further £100,000 for the Queen, Caroline of Ansbach. His rival, Sir Spencer Compton, had been cultivating the King's mistress Henrietta Howard, but Walpole had worked out that Henrietta exercised no political influence. Compton, he later commented, 'took the wrong sow by the ear'.

The farmyard phrase epitomised the country squire image on which Walpole built his career, playing the hard-riding, hard-drinking man of the soil for the sake of the landed gentry who voted with him year after year in the Commons. In reality, he was a sophisticated urbanite who built up a fabled art collection – his grandson sold the best of it to Catherine the Great of Russia – and he could skip around a balance sheet with the skill of any City merchant. He was a particular believer in the new science of statistics. Those who analysed Walpole closely called him the 'skreenmaster', because he hid the truth behind a plausible screen.

BORN AGAIN

1738

YOUNG JOHN WESLEY HAD NOT WANTED TO go to the Bible-study meeting being held beside the old wall of the city of London one evening in May 1738. But as the 34-year-old clergyman listened to a reading from the works of Martin Luther, he realised that he was deeply stirred: 'about a quarter before nine . . . I felt my heart strangely warmed. I felt I did trust in Christ, Christ alone for salvation, and an assurance was given me that He had taken away my sins, even mine.'

John Wesley's 8.45 revelation would inspire him to take Christianity to the thousands of dispossessed and down-trodden in Georgian England – and to do so with passion.

Strong feeling was not the religious style of the day. The Church of England was taking a rest after its centuries of upheaval. Anglican ministers, many of them relaxed and quite worldly gentlemen, dispensed the comforts of the faith to congregations for whom worship was often a matter of habit rather than burning conviction. Few vicars viewed the working classes as their priority, while the very shape and extent of their parishes, formed by the population patterns of pre-industrial England, would make it difficult for them to minister to the new mining and manufacturing communities that were soon to spring up all over the country.

It was to reach these people that John Wesley rode out into the fields in the early summer of 1739. In a series of over 150 outdoor meetings between April and June he set fire to the new 'Methodist' movement, so called after the attempts that John and his brother Charles, another clergyman, had made together at Oxford when they formed the 'Holy Club', its aim to practise what they saw as the 'methods' of the early Church – to pray and read together, to fast, to make regular confession, to visit prisoners in jail.

To these the energetic John added travelling. In the remaining fifty-two years of his life, the wiry five-foot-three-inch evangelist trekked some 4000 miles annually on horseback – a total of 208,000 miles (over 330,000 kilometres) – preaching at least two sermons a day, and frequently four or five, to congregations whose only shelter from the weather was often the foliage of a tree overhead.

Legend would trace Wesley's sense of mission back to a providential escape in his childhood when fire demolished his family's Lincolnshire home. As his parents realised with horror that John, the fifteenth of nineteen children, had been left inside, the six-year-old miraculously appeared at an upstairs casement window and was rescued seconds before the flaming roof collapsed. He was 'a brand plucked from the burning', and his followers took this as a metaphor for their own God-given salvation. Methodist lay preachers did not need to be ordained at Oxford or anywhere else: they were qualified simply by their ability to preach. And women played a prominent role in the movement.

The Church correctly viewed Wesley's preaching as subversive. It undermined their monopoly of the pulpit as he took his message to the poverty-stricken communities of London, Bristol, the Midlands and the north. In fact, his message was not subversive, nor was it revolutionary. Wesley himself tried to work within the Anglican communion – it was only after his death that the Methodists split from the Church of England – and he did not call directly for social change. But his 'Second Reformation' revived Martin Luther's exciting idea that a man could communicate directly with his God, finding new purpose in life through the vigour of spiritual rebirth – and this inspiring notion would, in due course, make its impact on social rebirth as well. The working-class movements of the nineteenth century owed much to the ethos of Methodism and the chapel. John Wesley would have shuddered, but he was one of the godfathers of socialism.

DICK TURPIN – 'STAND AND DELIVER!'

1739

A FEW DAYS BEFORE HE WAS DUE TO BE executed, the highwayman Richard Turpin bought himself a new frock-coat and smart new footwear – he was planning to meet his death in style. The most wanted criminal in England had hired himself five mourners to escort him to the gallows, and as the cart carried him through the crowd that gathered on the outskirts of York, he bowed ceremoniously to left and right.

Turpin had spent his last days in prison entertaining visitors with jokes and drinks. Now, on Saturday 7 April, 1739, he climbed the ladder of the 'three-legged mare', the triangular gallows on York racecourse, stamping his left leg to subdue a tremor that betrayed his fear. The noose was placed around his neck and he spoke briefly to the executioner whose job it was to pull the ladder away. But the victim did the hangman's work for him. The frock-coated highwayman jumped boldly off the ladder – 'dying with as much intrepidity and unconcern,' according to one eyewitness, 'as if he had been taking [a] horse to go on a journey'.

Highwaymen were the bane of travellers in Georgian England, flourishing to the end of the eighteenth century. With the bank transfer system in its infancy, many people travelled with bags containing quite substantial sums of cash. Policing was primitive, and passengers on the stagecoaches that started operating in the early 1730s dreaded the thunder of hooves, the juddering pull to a halt and the cry, 'Your money or your life!'

Some of the earliest, mid-seventeenth-century highway robberies were carried out by renegade royalist army officers, and it may have been their cavalier style that inspired the legend of the highwayman as a latter-day Robin Hood. Balladeers and poets built on the idea of the gentleman footpad who treated his victims with gallantry, particularly when it came to the fairer sex.

But the record shows that the average highwayman was simply a mugger on horseback – and Dick Turpin was proof of that. A heavily pockmarked man with a vile temper and a penchant for brutality, he was a member of the notorious Essex Gang who specialised in raiding and terrorising remote farmhouses on the outskirts of London. In the course of their housebreaking, they tortured one old man of seventy and raped a servant girl at pistol point. Turpin himself held a defenceless elderly woman over an open fire until she revealed where the family savings were hidden – and it was only when his fellow gangsters were brought to justice in 1735 that he turned to highway robbery south of the Thames.

The thug was brought down by his temper. When London got too hot for him Turpin went north, where he settled in Yorkshire and survived undetected under the pseudonym of 'John Palmer' – until he got into a quarrel with his landlord, shooting his prize farmyard cockerel and threatening to kill the landlord too. The man complained and Palmer/Turpin was arrested.

The death of Richard Turpin was the subject of one contemporary pamphlet, but otherwise the criminal died unlamented – one among the thousands strung up on the gallows of Georgian England for offences ranging from petty theft to murder. But a century later the novelist William Harrison Ainsworth devised the story of a Yorkshire country gentleman, one Jack Palmer, who lived a secret life as a highwayman. Ainsworth had clearly read the account of Palmer/Turpin's last days in Yorkshire, and to this he added other tales, notably the account that Daniel Defoe wrote in the 1720s of a dramatic ride from London to York by an earlier highwayman, 'Swift Nicks'.

In 1834 Ainsworth brought these different sources together in his bestselling romance *Rookwood*, which treated his readers to a dashing account of Dick Turpin riding north on his beloved mare, to whom the novelist, probably drawing on a ballad of 1825, gave the name Black Bess: '[Turpin's] blood spins through his veins, winds round his heart, mounts to his brain. Away! Away! He is wild with joy . . . A hamlet is visible in the moonlight . . . A moment's clatter upon the stones and it is left behind.'

Ainsworth made the imaginary Black Bess the faithful heroine of his story, vividly describing how she gamely kept her master ahead of the chasing posse, and only sank to her knees when she had finally carried him to safety: 'Bess tottered, fell. There was a dreadful gasp – a parting moan – a snort; her eye gazed for an instant upon her master with a dying glare . . . a shiver ran through her frame. Her heart had burst.'

The first edition of *Rookwood* sold out rapidly and was reprinted in August that year. 'Dauntless' Dick Turpin and his mare soon became the subject of popular prints and illustrations, and it was not long before authenticating anecdotes sprang up along the Great North Road, where innkeepers related how Turpin had refreshed his brave mount with ale – they could even produce the ancient tankard from which Black Bess had drunk. Here was the gully she had cleared in one stride, there was the five-bar tollgate she had vaulted with ease – Dick Turpin and the gallant black mare he never rode had passed into history.

GOD SAVE THE KING!

1745

God save our noble King!
God save Great George our King!
God save the King!
Send him victorious,
Happy and glorious,
Long to reign o'er us,
God save the King.

WHEN THESE WORDS WERE SUNG IN public for the first time in September 1745, the anxious crowd that filled the London theatre rose to their feet,

clapping wildly and calling for encores. Various versions of the
song had been around for some time, in praise of a number of
kings – the deposed James II among them. But on this warm
autumn evening, the song was addressed to the Hanoverian
monarch of the moment, George II, and the words were
sung with special fervour. It was effectively a prayer, since at
that moment 'Great George, our King' really did stand in
need of saving – along with the audience and all those whose
interests were linked to the survival of the German
Protestant dynasty.

That July, the 24-year-old grandson of James II, Charles
Edward Stuart, the Young Pretender, whose aim was to make
himself King Charles III, had landed in Scotland. Through
August the clans had rallied to his cause, and in September
the Highlanders marched on Edinburgh. Even as anxious
Londoners were singing 'God Save the King!' the Scottish
capital was going Stuart. Twenty-thousand excited citizens
cheered the claimant into the city, shouting out the romantic
nickname by which the Prince would be known to history –
'Bonnie Prince Charlie'.

Fine-featured and willowy with rosebud lips and limpid
brown eyes, Charles Edward Stuart was bonny indeed.
Born and brought up in Rome by his father the Old
Pretender, who had made his own bid for the throne in
1715, Charles Edward Stuart spoke three languages (English,
French and Italian), and had a roster of accomplishments
that included riding, shooting, royal tennis, shuttlecock
(modern badminton), dancing, golf and playing the cello.
He also had the knack of bearing himself like a king:
he looked particularly magnificent when wearing a kilt and

marching amongst the ranks, kicking up dust and mud with his men.

The Young Pretender had a streak of daring that brought him early success. He had set off on his adventure against his father's advice, and once he had secured his position in Edinburgh he headed his army south, marching down the west coast to outflank the English army and capture the towns of Carlisle, Manchester, Preston and Wigan. By 4 December 1745 the five-thousand-strong Stuart army was in Derby – just 127 miles from London, which was defended at that moment by no more than two thousand regular troops plus local trained bands who had hurriedly gathered at Finchley.

With a quick dash south Bonnie Prince Charlie and his Highlanders could possibly have reached the capital ahead of George II's second son, the Duke of Cumberland, who was commanding the English army. Householders along the road from Derby to London started burying their gold, and in London itself there was a run on the banks on 'Black Friday', 4 December, as people withdrew their gold and silver. The King himself loaded a yacht with his treasures: God save the King indeed – and his riches too!

At this crucial moment, however, Charles Edward Stuart could not persuade his Scottish officers to march any further south. He had promised them armed support from France that had not been forthcoming, and – more serious – the local response had been depressing. As in 1715, English and Welsh Jacobites had chosen to stay at home rather than risk their lives and livelihood by rallying to the Stuart banner. Lacking funds, the Prince could only pay his men in food, and they were hankering for home. Reluctantly, Bonnie

Prince Charlie turned his march back towards Scotland, with the Duke of Cumberland shadowing his retreat.

The showdown came on Culloden Moor in the Highlands the following April, where Cumberland's superior artillery and cavalry pulverised the tired and hungry Stuart army. Bonnie Prince Charlie headed for the Western Isles with a price of £30,000 on his head, but no one betrayed him: for six months he eluded his red-coated pursuers, thanks to loyalists like Flora MacDonald who ferried him to safety on the island of Skye – whence he could make good his escape to France.

'Speed bonnie boat like a bird on the wing, over the sea to Skye,' ran the song. 'Carry the lad that's born to be king over the sea to Skye.'

To this day, the poignant ballad enshrines Scotland's yearning for its bonnie Prince – while down south 'God Save the King' enjoyed a career of its own, becoming the melody that bands struck up to mark a royal appearance. When in 1788, forty-three years after the '45, the writer Fanny Burney accompanied George II's grandson, George III, on a trip to Cheltenham to take the waters, she reported how 'every five miles or so there were bands of the most horrid fiddlers scraping "God save the King" with all their might, out of tune, out of time and all in the rain'.

By the 1800s the song had become so established as the expression of patriotic sentiment that it became accepted as the 'national anthem' – the world's first, which other countries hastened to copy. Prussia, Denmark, Switzerland, Russia and even the United States adopted the melody of 'God Save the King' for a period, setting it to words of their own. Later they preferred to sing their own song. But to this day, when the England soccer team line up to play the tiny principality of Liechtenstein, the same tune gets repeated – so good they play it twice.*

*The playing of 'God Save the Queen' reflects the confusion as to whether the inhabitants of the British Isles are primarily British or, more fundamentally, English, Irish, Scottish or Welsh. Their sporting teams tend to prefer their own local anthems, 'Land of Our Fathers' (Wales), 'The Soldier's Song' (Ireland) and 'Flower of Scotland', with England's supporters favouring 'Jerusalem', 'Land of Hope and Glory' (at the Commonwealth Games) and, recently, at rugby matches, the African-American gospel hymn 'Swing Low, Sweet Chariot', originally sung in homage to the hat-trick of tries scored against Ireland in 1988 by Chris Oti, England's first black player for eighty years. When it comes to the Olympic Games, however, it is 'God Save the Queen' to which all British athletes stand to attention – and sometimes cry.

DR JOHNSON'S DICTIONARY

1755

BY THE MIDDLE OF THE EIGHTEENTH CENTURY
Britain had a fair claim to being in the forefront of
Europe's economic, scientific and political progress.
Culturally, however, there was a void. While Italy had long
boasted its own dictionary, the *Vocabulario degli Accademici
della Crusca*, and France had *Le Dictionnaire de l'Académie
française*, England had no almanac of its vibrant and expand-
ing language. In 1746 a group of London publishers pooled
resources to correct the omission, entrusting the making of
a national dictionary to Samuel Johnson, an opinionated
36-year-old journalist of untidy appearance with a gift for
creating extremely neat definitions. Angling, he once said,

was 'a stick and a string, with a worm on one end and a fool on the other'.

The son of a struggling bookseller from Lichfield in Staffordshire, Johnson suffered in his childhood from scrofula, a tubercular disease of the lymph nodes contracted through infected milk. Popular belief held that the characteristic swellings, known as the 'King's Evil', responded to the royal touch, and in March 1712 the two-year-old Samuel was taken down to London by his mother to be 'touched' by Queen Anne in one of the last of these ceremonies ever held. For the rest of his life Johnson wore round his neck the gold 'touch piece' the Queen gave him, but he was not blessed with a cure. A subsequent operation to remove the swellings left his neck visibly scarred.

Also pockmarked with smallpox, Johnson was tall and stout with a curious stoop – 'almost bent double,' commented the writer Fanny Burney. 'His mouth is almost constantly opening and shutting as if he were chewing. He has a strange method of frequently twirling his fingers and twisting his hands. His body is in constant agitation, see-sawing up and down.'

Modern experts have diagnosed Johnson's grunts and head-rollings as St Vitus' Dance or Tourette's Syndrome. His friends knew the kindly spirit behind this intimidating exterior, and nicknamed him 'Ursa Major' – the Great Bear – revelling in his sharp wit. 'Let me see,' he once remarked, when reminded that the French Academy's forty members had taken forty years to compile their dictionary, while he was planning to write his, alone, in only three. 'Forty times forty is sixteen hundred. As three to sixteen hundred, so is the proportion of an Englishman to a Frenchman.'

In the event the task took him nine years. Working with five assistants who scribbled away in the attic of his home on the north side of Fleet Street, he produced definitions of more than forty-two thousand words, laced from time to time with his own wit and prejudice:

> . . . *Lexicographer.*   A writer of dictionaries, a harmless drudge.
>
> *Oats.*   A grain which in England is generally given to horses but in Scotland supports the people.

The dictionary was an instant success, republished in many editions, and Johnson was honoured with academic distinctions – Oxford University made him a Master of Arts and Dublin gave him a doctorate. As 'Dr Johnson', he became the great man of letters of his time, founding, with the painter Joshua Reynolds, 'The Club', whose members included the playwright and novelist Oliver Goldsmith, the orator Edmund Burke, the actor David Garrick and the biographer James Boswell, whose famous *Life of Johnson* has preserved many of the great man's sayings for posterity: 'patriotism is the last refuge of a scoundrel', 'when a man knows he is to be hanged in a fortnight it concentrates his mind wonderfully' – and his comment on the contracting of a second marriage after an unhappy first one, 'the triumph of hope over experience'.

Johnson's own marriage to Tetty, a widow twenty years his senior, was a love match, and after her death he filled his home with an eccentric ménage of oddballs: the blind and bad-tempered poet Anna Williams; an unlicensed surgeon, Robert Levet, along with a former prostitute named Poll, all tended by a black servant, Frank Barber, who had arrived as a boy from Jamaica. Johnson cared for them all, and developed a fierce aversion to the business of slavery. 'Here's to the next insurrection of the negroes in the West Indies,' was one of his toasts.

Johnson's robust views do not always square with the standards of today. 'A woman's preaching,' he declared, 'is like a dog walking on its hind legs. It is not done well but you are surprised to find it done at all.' But his honesty disarmed criticism. Confronted one day by an indignant complainant who demanded how, in his dictionary, he could have defined 'pastern' (a horse's ankle) as a horse's 'knee', he offered no excuse – 'Ignorance, madam, pure ignorance.'

GENERAL WOLFE AND THE
CAPTURE OF QUEBEC

1759

The curfew tolls the knell of parting day,
The lowing herd wind slowly o'er the lea,
The ploughman homeward plods his weary way,
And leaves the world to darkness, and to me.

GENERAL JAMES WOLFE WAS FAR FROM
home on the night of 12–13 September 1759 as he
quietly read the opening lines of Thomas Gray's *Elegy
Written in a Country Churchyard*. The general was with his
officers in a flat-bottomed boat, according to the young
midshipman who later recounted the tale, drifting under

cover of darkness down the ebb tide on Canada's St Lawrence River.

'I can only say, gentlemen,' declared Wolfe (who was not widely known as a poetry lover), 'that if the choice were mine, I would rather be the author of these verses than win the battle that we are to fight tomorrow morning.'

After months of inconclusive sparring, the British general had decided on a daring stroke to outwit the Marquis de Montcalm, commander of the troops defending Quebec, the capital of French Canada. By the light of a pale quarter-moon, the British general had embarked his 4600 red-coated soldiers on a flotilla of vessels that made their way silently downriver with muffled oarstrokes – to land at the foot of cliffs so steep that the French had not seriously fortified them.

As Scottish troops scrambled up the cliffs, a French sentry challenged them. Fortunately the leading Highlander was able to reply in convincing French, and his companions scrambled over the clifftop to surprise the hundred or so guards, most of whom were asleep. As dawn rose on the Heights of Abraham, the flat green plateau extending to the walls of Quebec, Montcalm was confronted by no less than seven battalions of British soldiers drawn up in order, ready to attack.

The battle for Quebec was part of the Seven Years War (1756–63), later described by Winston Churchill as the first ever 'world' war, since Britain, allied in Europe with Prussia, spread her battles with France, Russia, Spain and Austria beyond Europe and the Mediterranean to India, Africa, North America, the Pacific and the Caribbean. James Wolfe had learned his soldiering as an officer in the army of the Duke of

Cumberland, seeing action in 1746 at Culloden, then playing his part in the merciless subduing of the Scottish Highlands that followed. Self-assured, flamboyant, and almost manic in his will to win, Wolfe was once accused of madness by George II's Prime Minister, the Duke of Newcastle.

'Mad, is he?' retorted the King. 'Then I hope he will bite some others of my generals.'

The high-flying 33-year-old got engaged to be married shortly before he embarked for Canada in 1759, and his fiancée Katherine Lowther presented him with a sixpenny copy of Thomas Gray's *Elegy* as a going-away present. Gray was the most popular poet of the age: his reverie among the gravestones of a country churchyard, 'far from the madding crowd', had caught the imagination of a society that, now on the cusp of industrialisation, was coming to value the countryside it had once taken for granted. 'Full many a flower is born to blush unseen,' ran one couplet, 'And waste its sweetness on the desert air.'

Wolfe himself was anything but a shrinking violet – so cocky and disdainful, in fact, that he was barely on speaking terms with many of his principal officers. His reference to 'the battle that we are to fight tomorrow morning' was the first that some of them had heard of his plan. He was also capable of indecision. When he got to the top of the cliff with an early wave of soldiers, he seems to have lost his nerve, according to one source, and impulsively sent down an order to unload no more soldiers in the cove.

But down on the beach his officers kept the boats coming – and up on the Heights of Abraham the French panicked. Instead of waiting for reinforcements who might have outflanked the exposed line of redcoats, Montcalm attacked in a rush. As his Canadian irregulars advanced, they were mown down by British musket-fire, and Montcalm himself sustained a fatal wound to his stomach.

By this stage of the battle, Wolfe also lay dying, shot down after he had stood on a rise in clear view and easy range of the enemy. The general had been ill for weeks, suffering severe bladder pains. High on opium, he was also weakened by bloodletting, the primitive duo of remedies that his physicians had prescribed for his fever and his tubercular cough, and it was hardly surprising if his behaviour was erratic. The evidence suggests that James Wolfe may have deliberately exposed himself to danger on the Heights of Abraham, knowing that he did not have long to live.

The general received the hero's death that he had yearned for – immortalised some years later by Benjamin West's epic painting *The Death of General Wolfe*. The capture of Quebec crowned a year of triumphs in a war that would lay the foundations of Britain's overseas empire, and the victor's embalmed body was honoured with a glorious state funeral and burial in Westminster Abbey. Wolfe's will gave instructions that five hundred guineas be spent on framing the portrait of his fiancée with jewels as his farewell present to her, and among his personal effects was the copy of Gray's *Elegy* that had been Katherine's parting gift. The little booklet reposes today in the archives of Toronto University, where you can see the underlinings the general made while he was planning the daring coup that brought him fame and victory. One underlining seems especially poignant: 'The paths of glory lead but to the grave.'

JAMES HARGREAVES AND THE
SPINNING JENNY

1766

FOR CENTURIES THE SPINNING WHEEL STOOD in the corner of almost every hearth in England – the basis of the country's cottage industry. Whenever she had a spare half-hour or so, the woman (and quite often the man) of the house would sit down at the ungainly contraption to tease out raw wool into skeins that could then be sold for weaving. After the discovery of the Americas, it was often cotton wool that went on to the spindle, with merchants supplying bundles of the fluffy raw material to cottage spinners whom they paid under the 'putting-out' system to supply them with the finished thread. Many spinners were also weavers.

By the mid-eighteenth century the damp and industrious northwestern county of Lancashire was a major centre of this domestic cotton production, and one day in the 1760s an overturned spinning wheel inspired James Hargreaves, a hand-loom weaver from the village of Oswaldtwistle, to devise a way of dramatically increasing production. Hargreaves was struck by the way that the overturned wheel kept on spinning – as did the usually horizontal spindle.

What would happen, the weaver wondered, if several spindles were to be placed upright, side by side? Might it not be possible to spin several threads at once? Working with a knife, Hargreaves shaped a primitive engine, or 'jinny', a single spinning wheel, with, eventually, as many as eight separate spindles.

The 'spinning jenny' (finally perfected, according to his daughter Mary, in 1766) turned ordinary cottage kitchens into mini-workshops – and the initial reaction from some was distrust. Angry neighbours raided Hargreaves' barn and burned the first twenty jennies he had built – on the grounds, according to Mary, that the machines would 'ruin the country'. If one jenny could do the work of eight spinners, reasoned the neighbours, that would put seven out of work.

In fact, the spectacular new spinning capacity of the Lancashire cottages and barns provided the basis for a cotton boom. The county became the English centre of cotton cloth production in the 1760s and 70s, turning out not just rough calicoes but delicate muslins, and as earnings rose, spinners and weavers took to parading the streets on paydays with £5 notes in their hatbands. Their wives drank tea out of the finest china.

The fine but tough yarns needed for these new fabrics were made possible by a host of mechanical innovations. Richard Arkwright, a barber and wigmaker from Preston, worked with a Warrington clockmaker, John Kay, to produce a 'frame' which used rollers to draw out and twist the yarn. Samuel Crompton, a Bolton weaver, devised a crossbreed of the jenny and frame that became known as the 'spinning mule'.

Edmund Cartwright, a poet-clergyman, thought he was enhancing this golden age of pastoral prosperity when he invented a power-loom operated by a caged bull that turned a huge treadmill. But bull power was soon supplanted by steam power, and by the end of the eighteenth century the old putting-out system was doomed. Steam- and water-powered workshops and factories could mass produce ever cheaper cotton thread and cloth. By 1801, the painter Joseph Farington was to note in his diary: 'In the evening I walked to Cromford [Derbyshire], and saw the children coming from their work out of one of Mr Arkwright's factories. These children had been at work from 6 or 7 o'clock this morning and it is now 7 in the evening.' The dark satanic mill had been created.

Lecturing on these events in the 1880s, the Oxford scholar and social reformer Arnold Toynbee coined the phrase 'Industrial Revolution' to describe the economic transformation of England that started in the 1760s. But modern scholars dispute this impression of dramatic upheaval, pointing out the gradual and incremental nature of the process that went from Hargreaves to Arkwright and Kay, from Samuel Crompton to Cartwright, and then on to James Watt, who modified Newcomen's engine (see p. 24) to bring steam power into the process – the Industrial Evolution, in fact.

CAPTAIN COOK – MASTER OF
THE PILOTAGE

1770

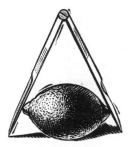

THE SECRET OF GENERAL WOLFE'S DARING capture of Quebec in 1759 was navigation – the mastery that the British navy achieved over the shoals of the treacherous St Lawrence River. 'The enemy has passed 60 ships of war where we hardly dared risk a vessel of 100 tons,' grumbled the French second-in-command, the Marquis de Vaudreuil, as he watched the British navigate their way upriver that June – and the star of those navigators was a thirty-year-old ship's master from Yorkshire, James Cook. Following the capture of Quebec, the young officer was awarded a special bonus of £50 (£5690 today) for 'indefatigable industry' in making himself the 'master of the pilotage'.

James Cook came from humble origins. The son of a Yorkshire farm labourer, he started work as a shop assistant before joining the crew of a dirty broad-bottomed colliery ship that transported coal from Tyneside down to London. For eleven years he learned his seamanship by battling the storms and shifting sandbanks of the North Sea, before he enlisted in 1755, aged twenty-six, as an ordinary sailor in the Royal Navy. In just two years, Able Seaman Cook took his Master's exams, qualifying himself 'to observe all coasts, shoals, and rocks, taking careful notes of the same'.

Cook had had only a few years of basic schooling at his home village of Whitby, so he spent his spare time at sea educating himself in Greek, mathematics and astronomy. After the conquest of Quebec he helped compile a chart of the Gulf of St Lawrence and spent much of the 1760s surveying the north and west coasts of Newfoundland. Every summer for five years he sailed and measured these chilly North Atlantic waters before returning to England to spend the winter drawing up his meticulous charts. Then, in 1768, came the invitation to participate in the 'greater Undertaking' – a scientific mission to measure the sun's distance from the earth, plus a secret mission from the King.

Venus was due to pass across the sun in June 1769, and the scientists of the Royal Society knew that the sun's location could be worked out by measuring the planet's passage from three different points on the globe. Lieutenant Cook, who was by now the navy's top navigational expert, was allocated the South Pacific leg of the experiment, setting sail on 25 August 1768 in the *Endeavour*, a sturdy, round-bottomed collier from his native Whitby. On board were eleven scientists, including the Eton-educated botanist Sir Joseph Banks, who was to become Cook's lifelong friend and supporter.

Only after the astronomical observation of June 1769 did Cook open his sealed orders – to steer onwards and locate, once and for all, the fabled Terra Australis, literally 'the land of the south' which Dutch navigators had first logged a century earlier. On 29 April 1770 the *Endeavour* put down anchor just south of modern Sydney in a cove that Cook named Botany Bay, after the large number of unusual plant species that Joseph Banks located there.

Banks himself was not complimentary. 'It resembled in my imagination the back of a lean cow,' he wrote of the weathered landscape, 'covered in general with long hair, but nevertheless where her scraggy hipbones have stuck out further than they ought, accidental rubbs and knocks have intirely bar'd them of their share of covering.'

Cook claimed this east coast of Terra Australis for George III, naming it New South Wales, before heading for England where he arrived in June 1771, almost three years after his departure. He had measured the passage of Venus accurately and charted some 4400 miles of New Zealand and Australian coastline. But equally remarkable was his feat in getting his crew home without succumbing to the sometimes fatal disease of scurvy, the occupational hazard of long voyages that caused sailors' limbs to swell and their gums to rot.

Twenty years earlier a Scottish doctor, James Lind, had established that scurvy – essentially vitamin C deficiency – could be prevented by the consumption of fresh lemon and lime juice, but it wasn't until 1795 that Lind's rations (which eventually gave British sailors the nickname 'Limeys') were officially adopted by the navy. Cook's preference was for a concentrated vegetable gel known as portable soup, along with carrot marmalade and sauerkraut – pickled, fermented cabbage.

'Few men have introduced into their ships more novelties in the way of victuals and drink than I have done,' wrote Cook, describing how he got his crew to gather cabbage palms and wild celery in New Zealand – to their disgust. They condemned this vegetable fare 'as stuff not fit for human beings to eat'.

One local curiosity in which they did show interest was the Polynesian tradition of tattooing, which they first encountered on the island of Tahiti. With time on their hands, several sailors and the young nature artist, Sydney Parkinson, 'underwent the operation' and proudly brought their tattoos home, starting a naval tradition that would later become a fashion statement.

In subsequent voyages Cook crossed the Antarctic Circle three times and discovered the South Sandwich Islands. In Alaska he proved definitively that there was no Northwest Passage, before turning back via Hawaii – where, in a tragic skirmish with islanders over a stolen boat in 1779, he was clubbed to death on the beach. Isolated in an angry crowd, he had ordered his men to 'Take to the boats' that were floating off the rocky shore, but why he did not take to the water himself remains a mystery. Perhaps Captain Cook was too brave or too proud to flee. But there is another explanation: like a surprising number of sailors in the old Royal Navy, the great navigator had never learned how to swim.

THE BOSTON TEA PARTY

1773

IN DECEMBER 1773 THREE BRITISH MERCHANT ships lay at anchor in the harbour of Boston, Massachusetts, their holds filled with forty-five tons of tea. Packed in 342 wooden chests, there was enough of the dried leaf, it has been calculated, to brew twenty-four million cups of tea – and, offloaded from an overproduction in India, it was going at a bargain price.

Yet the tea seemed no bargain to the citizens of Boston who, for more than a decade, had been tussling with the British government over the troublesome question of tax. As London saw it, the two and a half million inhabitants of North America's thirteen colonies should pay for the protection provided by the British troops stationed there. But many Americans resented the meddling of a government that was three thousand miles away. In 1763, for instance, London had halted the colonists' land-grab of native 'Indian' territories by drawing the 'Proclamation Line' along the Appalachian Mountains, creating a boundary beyond which the colonists were forbidden to seize or purchase native land.

Over the years a succession of British governments had first imposed, then withdrawn, a variety of taxes and customs duties in the face of colonial non-compliance and opposition. But tea was the exception, retained by London less to raise revenue than to defend a point of principle. 'There must always be one tax to keep up the right,' declared King George III, who had succeeded his grandfather George II in 1760. 'And as such I approve of the tea duty.'

On the night of 16 December 1773, a group of fifty activists showed what they thought of the royal claim. Painting their faces with red ochre and lamp-black and dressing in blankets to disguise themselves as Indian warriors, these tomahawk-wielding 'Mohawks' boarded the three British merchantmen to smash open the tea chests and spill their cargoes into the waters of Boston harbour. Next morning, rowing-boats steered out into the brown slurry to push any still-floating cases under the water and make sure that the hated British tea was well and truly ruined.

'No taxation without representation!' declaimed Samuel Adams, the local brewer whose oratory had helped inspire the demonstration.

Britain's reaction to Boston's act of defiance was split. Lord Chatham, who, as William Pitt, had masterminded Britain's victories in the Seven Years War, counselled conciliation. He knew how difficult a long-distance quarrel with the colonies could prove, and he called for Britain to pull back from the dispute 'while we can, not when we must'. But George III and his Prime Minister, Lord North, felt that the colonists must be compelled to show more respect for the 'mother country'. So the port of Boston was closed and troops were sent to reinforce the garrison.

The colonists refused to be cowed. Money and supplies poured in to sustain the Boston population and local resistance forces were raised, the so-called minutemen who kept their weapons ready so they could fight the redcoats at a minute's notice. In April 1775 they clashed with British troops at the village of Lexington outside Boston. America's war with the mother country had begun.

On 4 July 1776 the representatives of all thirteen colonies gathered in Philadelphia as the 'United States', to pronounce their defiance in a Declaration of Independence. Most of its clauses recited their grievances and denounced George III – 'a prince whose character is marked by every act that may define a tyrant'. But the historic declaration is remembered today for the preamble which its framer, Thomas Jefferson, a radical young lawyer, drew from the thinking of John Locke: 'We hold these truths to be self-evident, that all men are created equal, but they are endowed by their Creator with certain inalienable rights, that among these are life, liberty and the pursuit of happiness.'

In the five years of war that followed, the colonists' forces were shrewdly led by George Washington, a Virginia landowner who had learned his fighting as a British officer during the Seven Years War. Far from home and fighting in impossible terrain, some of it dense forest, Britain's redcoats steadily lost ground – particularly after 1778 when France weighed in on the American side. It was the arrival of the French fleet in Chesapeake Bay in October 1781 that led to the final surrender of the British forces, who marched out of Yorktown to the tune 'The World Turned Upside Down'.

'Oh God,' declared Lord North when he received the news, 'it is all over.'

So America had won its liberty, creating a new republic in which all men were created equal – except for those who happened to be slaves. Four of the first five US presidents were slave-owners, including Washington and Jefferson.

'How is it that the loudest yelps for liberty,' asked Samuel Johnson derisively, 'come from the drivers of negroes?'

And then there was the plight of the new republic's pre-existing underclass, the native Americans. Independence meant the end of the Proclamation Line with which Britain had protected the enticing expanses of native territories. The white 'Mohawks' of the Boston Tea Party had borrowed the warpaint of the 'Red Indians'. Now they were free to take over their land.

THOMAS CLARKSON – THE
GIANT WITH ONE IDEA

1785

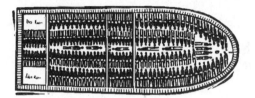

I own I am shocked at the purchase of slaves
And fear those who buy them and sell them are knaves.
What I hear of their hardships and tortures and groans
Is almost enough to draw pity from stones.
I pity them greatly, but I must be mum,
For how could we do without sugar and rum?

WILLIAM COWPER'S FLIPPANT POEM summed up most people's casual attitude to slavery in eighteenth-century England. Quakers were the exception – in 1774 all members of the Society of Friends agreed to have no dealings, personal or commercial, with slave-traders, and that same year John Wesley published an attack on slavery which helped swing Methodists against the commerce. By that date British slave-traders, sailing, for the most part, out of Bristol and Liverpool, had transported more than two million Africans across the Atlantic in conditions of unspeakable barbarity.

'I would do anything in my power,' Wesley later wrote, 'to the extirpation of that trade, which is a scandal not only to Christianity but to humanity.'

Then, in 1785, a young mathematics student at Cambridge University went in for a Latin essay competition. The topic was a philosophical question, '*Anne liceat invitos in servitutum?*' – 'Is it lawful to make men slaves against their will?' – and Thomas Clarkson won the prize for a hard-hitting essay in which he tackled the question in terms of 'the Slavery and Commerce of the Human Species, particularly the African'. Clarkson was invited to read out his work (in Latin) to an admiring audience in the university Senate House, then set out immediately for London on horseback 'meditating [as he later recalled] on the horrors of slavery all the way'.

'I frequently tried to persuade myself,' he wrote, 'that the contents of my essay could not be true.'

But the more he reflected on all the evidence he had studied, the more the mathematics graduate felt the impact of its depressing truth, and he was feeling particularly grim as he came in sight of Wade's Mill in Hertfordshire, about thirty miles into his sixty-mile journey. Giving his horse a rest, he was sitting down on the turf at the roadside, holding the reins disconsolately, when 'a thought came into my mind that, if the contents of the essay were true, it was time some person should see these calamities to their end'.

Clarkson decided that he should be that person. He had been planning a career in the Church. Now he decided to dedicate his life to the eradication of slavery. In 1786 he had his prize-winning essay published in English and next year convened, in a Quaker bookshop, the first meeting of the Committee for Effecting the Abolition of the Slave Trade. Headed by Clarkson, this twelve-man pressure group got Josiah Wedgwood, the great potter and social reformer, to devise for them a campaign badge that showed a manacled black slave on his knees, raising his chains to the motto: 'Am I not a man and a brother?'

The abolitionists' aim was an act of Parliament outlawing the trade, and in 1787 they recruited the Yorkshire MP William Wilberforce, who would become famous for his resolute championing of the cause in the initially hostile House of Commons. But the raw material of Wilberforce's speeches and the flood of local petitions that backed his Westminster campaign were largely the work of the indefatigable Clarkson, who mounted his trusty horse in the summer of 1787 and rode off for the slave port of Bristol. There he set to work gathering evidence, sitting in quayside taverns and persuading sailors to part with their 'souvenirs' – the manacles, whips and branding irons, along with the thumbscrews and forcible mouth-openers, that were the tools of the slavers' trade.

Then he headed north for Liverpool, where he picked up a particularly potent piece of propaganda – the plan of the local slave ship *Brookes*. Reprinted and widely circulated not just in Britain but in Europe and America, this graphic diagram showed how 609 slaves were crammed together, head to toe and side by side, on the notorious Middle Passage (see p.20). In the next seven years Clarkson would ride some thirty-five thousand miles setting up anti-slavery societies, making speeches – and risking his life as he recruited witnesses who could testify to the horrors of the profitable business. In Liverpool he narrowly escaped drowning at the hands of some enraged slavers.

When, after many battles and setbacks, the campaign to stop the slave trade finally triumphed in 1807, it was William Wilberforce who rightly received the credit for shepherding the Abolition Bill so tenaciously through Parliament. But it had been Thomas Clarkson who laid the groundwork, persuading 300,000 of the once apathetic British public to boycott sugar, and inspiring nearly 400,000 to sign petitions to Parliament. The prize-winning student who had got off his horse at Wade's Mill, then got back on and kept on riding, was, as the poet Samuel Taylor Coleridge put it, 'the moral steam engine' of the campaign to abolish slavery – 'the giant with one idea'.

THE MADNESS OF
KING GEORGE III

1788

IN AUGUST 1788 KING GEORGE III, FEELING ill, decided he should travel to the spa town of Cheltenham to take the waters. But although the bitter-tasting purgative water opened his bowels most effectively – he found 'a pint and a half the proper quantity to give him two openings' – his health did not improve. Walking the elegant streets with the Queen on his arm, he would raise his hat to total strangers as if they were dear old friends. The fifty-year-old King was suffering from agonising stomach pains and cramps in his legs. He found he could not concentrate on the letters he received from his Prime Minister, and he made numerous mistakes as his handwriting grew large and shaky. 'I'm afraid,' he said, 'Mr Pitt will perceive I am not quite in a situation to write at present.'

When he got back to London, the royal speech was slurred and his dress so disordered when he appeared in public that the Lord Chancellor, Lord Thurlow, felt he must advise His Majesty to go back to his closet to readjust his clothing. One day in chapel, the King stood bolt upright suddenly in the middle of the sermon and threw his arms around the Queen and his daughters.

'You know what it is to be nervous,' he cried. 'But was you ever as bad as this?'

As his agitation increased he could not stop talking, and though he told his attendants to keep him quiet by reading aloud to him, he kept on talking just the same. One day he fell on the shoulder of his 25-year-old son, the Duke of York. 'I wish to God I may die,' he cried out. 'For I am going to be mad!'

The future King George III had become heir to the throne at only twelve years of age, when his father Frederick Prince of Wales fell casualty to the newly fashionable game of cricket – struck on the head by a cricket ball and developing a fatal brain abscess. Nine years later, in 1760, the young king succeeded his grandfather George II, and set about making himself a hands-on monarch, proud to be the first of the Georges who was not brought up in Germany.

'Born and educated in this country,' he declared to the first Parliament of his reign, 'I glory in the name of Briton.'

Writing his own comments on the state papers and dating them to the day, hour and minute, George III was the last British king seriously to endeavour to rule the country himself. He believed that government should be directed by the Crown, not Parliament – but achieved exactly the opposite through his inflexible handling of the war against the American colonies. Determined to keep fighting after the British surrender at Yorktown in 1781, George was confronted by a clear majority in Parliament who wanted to sue for peace. His first reaction was to draft a letter of abdication. But on second thoughts, he decided to accept – and effectively obey – a Prime Minister, the Marquess of Rockingham, with whose policy he profoundly disagreed.

Modern experts have diagnosed the notorious 'madness' of George III as porphyria, 'the purple disease', so called because it turns its sufferers' urine deep red or purple. Mary Queen of Scots was said to have suffered from this rare disorder, which was hereditary and is presumed to have been passed down to George III through the Stuart line. Porphyrins are pigment cells, and an excess of these in the body leads to stomach cramps, constipation, rambling speech and hallucinations.

To counteract these symptoms, George's doctors resorted to a range of painful remedies that included blistering his shaven scalp and applying leeches to his forehead, to draw the poisonous matter from his brain. An alternative strategy sought to draw the bad humours down to the other end of his body by applying burning mustard plasters that opened wounds on his legs. Frequently confined in a straitjacket, with his arms tied round his back, the King was given strong purges then left in a room that was kept so cold that no one else could bear to stay in it for more than half an hour.

Not surprisingly enraged by these ordeals, the King

nevertheless preserved something of his sense of humour, describing the seat to which he was frequently strapped immobile as his 'coronation chair'. Attempting a drawing as he was recovering in January 1789, he commented, 'Not bad – for a madman.'

Modern treatments for porphyria include sedation, maintaining the balance of electrolytes in the body, a high carbohydrate diet and the avoidance of sunlight. Nothing in the treatments that George III received corresponds to modern medical practice, but somehow he began to recover in the early months of 1789, and, as he got better, it became clear that the drama of his tragic disorder as reported in the newspapers had transformed England's view of the previously unpopular King. 'Compassion for his late sufferings,' reported Fanny Burney, 'seems to have endeared him now to all conditions of men.' In 1810 the fiftieth anniversary of George's accession prompted bonfires, fireworks, feasting and the lighting of beacons all over the country – Britain's first ever royal jubilee.

By this date, however, the 72-year-old King was drifting once more into mental confusion, possibly a return of his porphyria, compounded by senility. For the last ten years of his life, his authority was exercised by his son, the future George IV, as Prince Regent. But before the old King slipped finally into the darkness, he went to visit a lunatic asylum at Richmond where he enquired about how inmates were treated and the use of the straitjacket. Catching sight one day of his own canvas costume of torture that had been left out by accident, he calmed his embarrassed equerry.

'You needn't be afraid to look at it,' he said. 'Perhaps it is the best friend I ever had in my life.'

'BREADFRUIT BLIGH' AND THE
MUTINY ON THE BOUNTY

1789

WHEN CAPTAIN COOK WAS KILLED IN Hawaii in 1779, one of the British officers charged with the grisly task of going from islander to islander, persuading them to hand back the dead hero's dismembered body parts, was Cook's 24-year-old sailing master, William Bligh. Having retrieved sufficient remains to carry out a burial at sea, Bligh then navigated his ship, the *Resolution*, north to the Bering Strait and back to England via Japan.

Before his death Cook had been examining the nutritional potential of a large, knobbly-skinned Polynesian fruit that had a sweet 'wheaten' taste – the breadfruit – and this provided the reason for the voyage that would make William

Bligh famous. The breadfruit was a staple of the Pacific islanders' diet, and Cook noted how the climate and latitude of Owhyhee (as he called it) 'differs very little from that of the West India islands'. Why not transplant the breadfruit tree to the Caribbean, where it could provide cheap fodder for slaves, especially as the recent war with the colonies had cut off food supplies from America?

In 1786 the Society of Arts announced a prize and a gold medal for the first person to 'convey six breadfruit plants' from the South Seas to the West Indies, and Cook's friend the botanist Sir Joseph Banks put forward Bligh's name. HMAV* *Bounty* was elaborately modified into a floating greenhouse with two large skylights, three large air vents on each side, a rainwater irrigation system and a false floor cut full of holes to contain the plants for the nine-month voyage – His Majesty's Armed Potting Shed.

On 23 December 1787, the *Bounty* set sail for the Pacific via Cape Horn, with Fletcher Christian, an old friend of Bligh's, serving as master's mate. The two men had both risen from the ranks and had got to know each other on a previous ship, HMS *Cambridge*, where Bligh taught Christian how to navigate and had dined with him frequently. In his diary Christian claimed that Bligh treated him 'like a brother'.

Bligh ran a relaxed ship by the harsh standards of the time. He hired a fiddler to keep up the spirits of the crew and organised jig-dancing between five and eight every evening. 'Cheerfulness with exercise,' was his recipe for beating scurvy, along with Captain Cook's favoured diet of dried malt,

*His Majesty's Armed Vessel.

sauerkraut and portable soup. But Bligh also had a temper,* and this was stretched when storms delayed the *Bounty*'s arrival in Tahiti. The breadfruit trees were now in their fruiting season and could not be transplanted for another five and a half months.

It must have seemed a good idea, after the rigours of the storm-tossed ten-month voyage, to let the crew of the *Bounty* relax in the luxuriant tropical surroundings of Tahiti. But here the seeds of the famous mutiny were sown – sun, sandy beaches, surf and, above all, affection and sex with the welcoming local women: after five and a half months of tropical tenderness, what man in his right mind would want to subject himself to the harshness of an eighteenth-century naval ship? By the time 1015 breadfruit plants had been potted up and placed in their slots in the floor of the Great Cabin on the *Bounty*, many of the crew had formed liaisons with local Tahitians whom they considered their 'wives'.

They lasted just three weeks at sea. On 27 April 1789, a fit of anger from Bligh over pilfered coconuts provoked Fletcher Christian and twenty-five of the crew to break open the ship's arms chest. Bligh was dragged from his bed and brought out on deck in his nightshirt with his hands tied. With seventeen crew members that remained loyal to him,

---

*Modern research has established that Captain Bligh flogged his sailors less than any other British commander in the Pacific Ocean in the late eighteenth century. But he had a vicious tongue. After one incident he showered his officers and crew with an array of insults – 'damn'd Infernal scoundrels, blackguard, liar, vile man, Jesuit, thief, lubber, disgrace to the service, damned long pelt of a bitch' – and he told them he would make them 'eat grass like cows'.

he was bundled into the *Bounty's* twenty-three-foot longboat and cast adrift with bread, water, salt pork, a little wine, four cutlasses, the carpenter's tool chest and a spare sextant.

From this point the story goes in several directions: the mutineers sailed back to be reunited with their 'wives' in Tahiti, where most elected to remain, sitting targets for the marines of HMS *Pandora* who were dispatched to arrest them in 1791. But Fletcher Christian and eight other mutineers sailed onwards in September 1789 with their Tahitian wives and six other islanders, to start a new life on the very outer limits of the known world, on the uninhabited island of Pitcairn. Here their descendants would eke out a bizarre and inbred existence, misfits to the present day.

Captain Bligh, meanwhile, carried out a feat of navigation and survival that remains unequalled in the annals of the sea. He piloted his open boat no less than 3600 miles (5800 kilometres) past the island of Fiji, along the uncharted north coast of Australia and across the Great Barrier Reef to Timor, the nearest European settlement. For forty-one days his eighteen men survived on such fish, turtles and seabirds as they could catch and eat raw, slaking their thirst on dribblings of rainwater.

Bligh returned home a hero, especially after he published his rapidly written *Narrative of the Mutiny on Board his Majesty's Ship Bounty*. After the formality of a court martial that cleared his name, the Admiralty sent him back to the South Seas on a voyage that did, finally, deliver several hundred breadfruit plants to the West Indies – as well as to the botanical gardens at Kew.

Bligh's subsequent career was curiously mutiny-prone. In

1797 he was captain of one of the several dozen warships that were taken over by their protesting crews in the massive mutiny at the Nore, the naval anchorage in the Thames near the Isle of Sheppey. In 1805 his attempts to clean up rum smuggling as governor of New South Wales pitched him against the corrupt local militia, who placed him under house arrest for more than a year. As before, an official inquiry exonerated him, and he became a respected vice-admiral, retiring to south London where his grave can be seen in the churchyard of St Mary-at-Lambeth.

According to his gravestone, William Bligh was famous as 'the celebrated navigator who first transplanted the bread-fruit tree from Otaheite to the West Indies, bravely fought the battles of his country, and died beloved, respected, and lamented'. There is no mention of the M-word.

But the mutiny, of course, is the entire reason why William Bligh has been commemorated by Hollywood. His dramatic showdown with Fletcher Christian has inspired no less than four movies graced by the talents of Errol Flynn (1933), Charles Laughton and Clark Gable (1935), Marlon Brando and Trevor Howard (1962) and Anthony Hopkins and Mel Gibson (1984). The supporting casts have included David Niven, James Cagney, Laurence Olivier, Daniel Day-Lewis, and Liam Neeson.

And all because he missed the breadfruit transplanting season.

THOMAS PAINE AND THE
RIGHTS OF MAN

1791

REPORTS OF THE SHOCKING EVENTS ON
board HMAV *Bounty* reached London as Britain was
digesting the news of an even greater convulsion – the
French Revolution. On 14 July 1789 enraged citizens had
stormed the Bastille, the sinister royal fortress that loomed
over eastern Paris. The stone-by-stone destruction of the
hated prison foreshadowed the fate of the French monarchy
itself in the months that followed, as Louis XVI and his
wife Marie-Antoinette fell victim to the fury of the *sans-
culottes* – literally, the trouserless ones – whose mob tactics
took control of the Revolution. Most British sympathies
were with the French royal family. But one Englishman,

Thomas Paine, was so enthused by events in France that he crossed the Channel to give the Revolution his active support.

Thomas Paine was captain of the awkward squad – provocative, eloquent and happy to offend anyone in defence of the libertarian principles he espoused. No respecter of persons, Paine head-butted the status quo in the great English tradition of Wat Tyler, the Levellers, and radicals to the present day. Born in 1737, the son of a Quaker corset-maker in Norfolk, he displayed his egalitarian principles in a poem he was said to have written at the age of eight:

Here lies the body of John Crow,
Who once was high but now is low.
Ye brother crows take warning all,
For as you rise, so must you fall.

News of trouble in the colonies in 1774 attracted Paine to America, where he settled in Philadelphia and soon made his name as a loudly anti-British campaigning journalist. 'As it is my design to make those who can scarcely read understand,' he later explained, 'I shall therefore avoid every literary ornament and put it in a language as plain as the alphabet.'

In the autumn of 1775 he published *Common Sense*, a hard-hitting pamphlet that sold more than a hundred thousand copies and became the clarion call of revolution. 'Government by kings,' he wrote, 'runs contrary to the natural equality of man . . . in America THE LAW IS KING.'

When George Washington's army suffered setbacks in 1776, Paine rallied the colonists' spirit. 'These are the times

that try men's souls,' he wrote in *The American Crisis*.
'Tyranny, like hell, is not easily conquered; yet we have this
consolation with us, that the harder the conflict, the more
glorious the triumph.'

Paine's private life was disorganised. He drank heavily
and took pride in his spectacularly unkempt appearance.
Suffering from scabies, the great polemicist stank from the
noxious ointments that he used to cure this pimply rash. He
was frequently in debt, and was happy to take employment
with the newly independent American government to fund
his erratic and extravagant lifestyle.

But Paine insisted that he served a higher cause. 'My principle is universal,' he wrote, 'my attachment is to all the
world' – and in 1789 he found a new cause to champion.
When Edmund Burke condemned the French Revolution,
Paine responded furiously with *The Rights of Man*, arguing
that it was not only France that suffered from its monarchy.

'It has cost England almost 17 millions sterling,' he wrote,
'to maintain a family imported from abroad, of very inferior
capacity . . . Hereditary governments are verging to their
decline and . . . revolutions on the broad basis of national
sovereignty and government by representation, are making
their way in Europe.'

The Rights of Man and *Common Sense* were the two best-
selling pamphlets of the eighteenth century, with an
international readership. In August 1792 Paine was one of
seventeen foreigners accorded the honour of French citizen-
ship, and the next month four of the revolutionary
départements elected him to represent them in the new
National Assembly. He chose to accept the invitation of

Calais, crossing the Channel to a rapturous reception. Guns fired as the champion of liberty was presented with a revolutionary cockade, and the streets were lined with people shouting, *'Vive Thomas Paine!'*. The mayor of Calais greeted him with a fervent embrace. 'I believe,' wrote one observer, 'he is rather fatigued with the kissing.'

When Paine reached Paris, however, and started work as a deputy, he found himself out of his depth. Speaking little French, he was lost in the rapid crossfire of revolutionary debate, and, deeply opposed to capital punishment, he found himself at odds with the fierce band of deputies who were intent on executing the King. 'France has been the first of European nations to abolish royalty,' he argued, through a translator, in his plea that Louis XVI be exiled to America. 'Let her also be the first to abolish the penalty of death.'

Paine's appeal was in vain. On 20 January 1793, the Convention narrowly voted that the ex-King should be dispatched to the guillotine, and as the death toll of 'the Terror' increased, the Englishman made no secret of his disenchantment. 'My friends were falling as fast as the guillotine could cut their heads off,' he later wrote to the Boston brewer, Samuel Adams, '. . . I expected, everyday, the same fate.'

At 4 a.m. on 28 December 1793 came the knock on his door. Assigned to the notorious prison of the Luxembourg, Paine succumbed to a fever that may have saved his life. Semi-conscious for several weeks, he was not fit enough to be herded into the carts of victims being transported to summary trial and execution – and then James Monroe, the American ambassador, intervened on his behalf. After nearly eleven months, Paine was finally released in November 1794 and taken to the safety of Monroe's Paris home.

It was impossible for the rebel to go home to England. In 1792 he had been tried in his absence and condemned as a traitor – a title that he proudly embraced. When, a few years later, he met the rising young general Napoleon Bonaparte (who claimed that he slept with a copy of *The Rights of Man* under his pillow), Paine was happy to discuss the prospects for an invasion of England, and even wrote two essays calling for a fleet of a thousand gunboats to carry French forces across the Channel. In 1802 he returned to America, his spiritual home, where he died seven years later.

Today his name still rouses passion. When the BBC recently screened a documentary in praise of Paine, the *Daily Telegraph* protested indignantly. 'He fought against his country in the American War of Independence and invited France to invade us during the French Revolution,' thundered an editorial, complaining that 'among decent Englishmen in his time his name was a synonym for treachery' – not to mention 'blasphemy' and 'debauchery'.

All this is true. But far bigger than his faults was Paine's inspiring big idea – that the rights of man, which include equality and liberty, are God-given at birth, and that governments are only good when they protect them.

MARY WOLLSTONECRAFT AND
THE RIGHTS OF WOMAN

1792

It is time to effect a revolution in female manners – time to restore them to their lost dignity – and make them as a part of the human species.

> *Mary Wollstonecraft,*
> Vindication of the Rights of Woman

RECIPES FOR CHANGING THE WORLD FLOWED from the presses during the 1790s. Inspired by the French Revolution, they made a torrent of passion-filled pamphlets, and until quite recently most historians felt that Tom Paine's *Rights of Man* held pride of place among them.

But as we have sought to explain how society is changing in our own times, we have come to focus more closely on a friend of Paine's whose visionary work was derided at the time and overlooked for nearly two centuries – Mary Wollstonecraft and her *Vindication of the Rights of Woman*.

'I am not born to tread in the beaten track,' declared this brave, insurgent and ultimately tragic woman who is now seen as the first modern feminist. On her birth in April 1759 she was handed over by her mother to be breast-fed by a 'wet nurse' – the normal practice in middle and upper-class families. Mary would criticise wet-nursing bitterly in later life: a mother's love, she wrote, 'scarcely deserves the name, when it does not lead her to suckle her children'. But she felt still more anger at the behaviour of her father Edward, a drunken and violent tyrant who lorded it over his womenfolk, beating Mary, bullying his wife, and wasting the family fortune on a succession of snobbish attempts to become a country gentleman. As a child Mary would sleep on the landing outside her mother's door in a vain attempt to protect her from Edward Wollstonecraft's alcohol-fuelled anger.

Wives were considered to be the property of their husbands in the eighteenth century. The marriage laws were, in effect, property laws that gave a man ownership of his wife, her money and her children: divorce was virtually impossible.

'How short a time does it take,' reflected Fanny Burney after spending a few hours at a friend's wedding in the 1780s, 'to put an eternal end to a woman's liberty?'

It was taken for granted that a man could beat his womenfolk – a court case of 1782 confirmed that beating was legal, provided the stick was no thicker than the man's thumb. And the idea that a woman of quality might want to work to support herself was dismissed as downright crazy.

Mary was a working woman, compelled by her father's improvidence to earn her living as a nurse, seamstress, schoolmistress, governess and eventually as a campaigning writer. In 1787 at the age of twenty-eight she published *Thoughts on the Education of Daughters* in which she argued (as a girl who had hated playing with dolls) that women should pursue the same serious studies as men. Education, in her view, was the key to self-respect and hence to female empowerment, the theme of her great work *A Vindication of the Rights of Woman*, which she wrote in six furious weeks in 1792. 'I wish,' she explained, 'to persuade women to endeavour to acquire strength, both of mind and body.'

Mary's *Vindication* fiercely disputed the idea that women were the weaker sex. They were not naturally inferior, she argued, but they had tricked themselves into seeing their life's duty as the pleasing of men. 'Confined . . . in cages like the feathered race', she wrote disdainfully, women were raised as fine 'ladies' rather than as capable workers, with 'nothing to do but plume themselves, and stalk with mock majesty from perch to perch'. She was particularly alert to 'the selfish vanity of beauty' and poured scorn on society women, trapped in their carriages 'that drive helter-skelter about this metropolis . . . pale-faced creatures who are flying from themselves'.

Published in England, Ireland, France, Germany and the USA, Mary's trenchantly argued *Vindication* provoked strong feelings. Horace Walpole, the gossipy youngest son of Sir Robert Walpole, denounced her as a 'hyena in petticoats'.

But radical thinkers like Tom Paine applauded her and welcomed her to Paris in 1792, when she arrived to write her own account of the French Revolution – which, as the twentieth-century champion of women's writing, Virginia Woolf, later wrote, was not merely an event to Mary. 'The revolution . . . was an active agent in her own blood. She had been in revolt all her life – against tyranny, against law, against convention.'

In Paris she met Captain Gilbert Imlay, a handsome American land speculator with whom she defied convention by embarking on a tempestuous love affair, bearing a daughter out of wedlock in May 1794. But the romance cooled, and returning to London, Mary discovered that Imlay had a mistress. In despair she rented a rowing-boat that took her to Putney, where she threw herself from the bridge, having walked up and down in the pouring rain for half an hour to drench her clothes and make sure she would sink.

Mary was rescued. The recently established Royal Humane Society was offering rewards to boatmen who foiled would-be suicides, and one of these dragged Mary from the water. The mixture of depression and resolve that characterised her suicide attempt ran right through her life. Volatile and self-dramatising, with a deep-rooted sense of personal grievance, she was emotionally fragile, but she kept on fighting the male-dominated conventions of her day. In her uncompleted novel *Maria, or the Wrongs of Woman*, she advanced the shocking assertion that a woman could have sexual desires that were as strong as a man's.

In 1797 Mary fell pregnant again, by William Godwin, a critic and reformer in whom she finally found a soulmate.

Godwin shared her contempt for marriage – Mary had condemned the institution as tyranny and legalised prostitution, deciding at the age of twelve that she would never marry and suffer her mother's fate. But she and Godwin married anyway, and enjoyed five months of happiness before Mary died that September, following the birth of another daughter.

This Mary, like her mother, would defy convention, running off with the poet Percy Bysshe Shelley and writing the myth-making novel *Frankenstein*, the story of a man who fashioned a creature that he thought he could control, but which escaped from his power and eventually destroyed him.

ENGLAND EXPECTS . . .

1805

WHEN HE SPOTTED A POLAR BEAR prowling the ice near the island of Spitzbergen in the Arctic Ocean, the fifteen-year-old Horatio Nelson leapt over the rail of his ship and went in pursuit with a musket. But the beast outmanoeuvred the skinny-legged midshipman, rearing up angrily over him, and when the boy pulled the trigger, nothing happened. His powder was wet. Seizing his gun by the barrel, Nelson was about to club his adversary around the head when a cannon shot rang out from the ship behind him. Startled by the cannonball, the bear slunk away.

'Sir,' declared the apprentice officer defiantly and

ungratefully to the captain who had saved him, 'I wished to kill a bear so that I might carry the skin to my father.'

This story from the youth of Admiral Lord Nelson sums up the man – fearless, single-minded, and just a little crazy. They were qualities Britain needed in the years between 1798 and 1805, when Nelson commanded the fleets that confronted Napoleon. By the time he fought the first of his great battles he had already lost his right arm and the sight of his right eye in action.

The evening of 1 August 1798 found Nelson at the mouth of the River Nile, where Napoleon had brought his armies for the conquest of Egypt. The French admiral Brueys did not believe that the British would actually attack – they had only just appeared over the horizon, and it was the end of the day. But Nelson's ships just kept on sailing hard at the enemy, starting to fire as dusk fell. The Battle of the Nile was fought in darkness, with the flashing broadsides of cannonfire eerily silhouetting the tussling ships.

'Nelson comes, the invincible Nelson!' the victorious admiral wrote proudly home to his wife Fanny. Already this 39-year-old was sometimes referring to himself in the third person. 'Almighty God has made me the happy instrument in destroying the enemy's fleet,' he wrote to Sir William Hamilton, the British ambassador at Naples.

The ambassador could hardly have imagined what would happen next. Landing in Naples on his way back from the Nile, Nelson fell hopelessly in love with Hamilton's wife Emma, an exuberant beauty who was famous for her 'Attitudes', posing in exotic and diaphanous costumes as if she were a figure on a classical Greek vase. The romance between Nelson and the glamorous Lady Hamilton became the talk of Europe, and though both remained married to their long-suffering spouses, in 1801 Emma bore Nelson a daughter whom they christened Horatia – a name not designed for secrecy.

Fiercely disapproving, King George III snubbed Nelson when he next met him, and Queen Charlotte made it clear that she would not receive Lady Hamilton at court. But Nelson's saucy love life only added to his celebrity status, which he cultivated to the hilt, glorying in his glittering array of medals and orders, and making sure that favourable accounts of his triumphs found their way into the newspapers.

The hero would surely have been delighted that the most famous anecdote about him – that he placed a telescope to his blind eye so as to ignore an order during the Battle of Copenhagen in 1801 – was a legend devised after his death. The detailed account by Colonel William Stewart who was standing beside him on the quarterdeck at the time makes clear that Nelson certainly did ignore a signal to leave off action. But his 'turning a blind eye' was not described until five years later (no contemporary picture shows him wearing an eye patch), and the detail of the telescope was added three years after that.

During his lifetime Nelson's charisma inspired intense loyalty in his sailors. 'Nelson is arrived,' wrote Captain Edward Codrington of HMS *Orion* in September 1805 when the admiral's black-and-yellow chequered flagship *Victory* joined the British fleet outside Cadiz. 'A sort of general joy has been the consequence.'

'Everything seemed, as if by enchantment, to prosper under his direction,' declared Cuthbert Collingwood, his second-in-command off the Spanish coast.

Inside Cadiz harbour lay the combined French and Spanish fleets, the key to Napoleon's hopes of invading England. So, as the enemy sailed out of Cadiz, their sails set for battle, the British admiral put his fleet on its mettle: 'Nelson confides [is confident],' ran the signal he drafted, 'that every man will do his duty.'

Someone suggested 'England' instead of 'Nelson', and Nelson happily passed that on to his flag lieutenant. But the signalling officer explained that 'confides' would need eight flags, while 'expects' could be broadcast with just three – and thus was transmitted, at 11.35 a.m. on 19 October 1805, the most famous battle signal in English history.

In the four-hour duel that followed, the British ships drove directly into the enemy line as they sailed past Cape Trafalgar. Grapeshot cut Nelson's secretary in half where he stood beside the admiral, and up in the rigging of one of the French ships a sniper lined his sights on the flamboyant, medal-emblazoned coat of the little British commander. The bullet broke Nelson's back, opened an artery, and entered his lung. 'They have done for me at last,' he gasped.

As he lay below decks in the medical cockpit, its walls painted red to camouflage the blood that splashed every-where, he asked why the sailors were cheering. Thomas Hardy, the flag captain of *Victory*, told him that fourteen or fifteen enemy ships had surrendered. 'That is well,' responded Nelson, 'but I had bargained for twenty.'

He knew that he was dying. 'Take care of my dear Lady

Hamilton,' he told his captain. 'Take care of poor Lady Hamilton. Kiss me Hardy.'

In later years the Victorians could not bear the idea that Nelson had asked another man to kiss him, and came up with the suggestion that he really said 'Kismet', from the Persian word for 'fate' or 'destiny'. But the account by the surgeon Dr Beatty was quite definite. Captain Hardy kissed the dying man twice – on the cheek and on the forehead.

FANNY BURNEY'S BREAST

1811

FANNY BURNEY DID NOT HEAR THE NEWS OF
Nelson's victory at Trafalgar until seven years after the
battle. Having married a French nobleman, the sprightly novelist had moved to France, where Napoleon had decreed that
all English people between the ages of eighteen and sixty
should be regarded as prisoners of war: they were forbidden
to write to, or receive letters from, their families in England.

We have already heard from Fanny Burney a couple of
times in these tales. She was a wise and wry observer of life
in George III's England, where her novels won high praise.
'Oh, you little character-monger you!' chuckled Dr Johnson,
giving her a squeeze after reading her first romance, *Evelina*.

Jane Austen, who was composing her own novels in these years, praised Fanny's books – 'in which the most thorough knowledge of human nature, the happiest delineation of its varieties, the liveliest of wit and humour, are conveyed to the world in the best chosen language'.

In 1793, at the age of forty-one, Fanny married the charming if penniless Alexandre d'Arblay, a royalist army officer who had fled the Revolution and was living in Surrey. So penniless was the ex-general that for weeks at a time the d'Arblays had to survive on nothing but the vegetables that he grew in the garden. The Peace of Amiens coaxed the family to Paris in 1802, hopeful of recovering the d'Arblay rank and property – Napoleon was looking for good officers, ex-royalists included. But the resumption of hostilities in May 1803 trapped Fanny in enemy territory, and for nearly a decade she lived in limbo.

Fanny Burney's novels are difficult to read today – their wordiness seems dated in a way that Jane Austen's style is not. But her personal journals and letters are often breathtaking in their sharp-eyed observation, and one agonising incident during her long French 'captivity' inspired some writing that has become a classic of medical history. In the summer of 1810 she started experiencing pains in her right breast and felt a lump that a gathering of eminent doctors diagnosed as cancerous.

'*Il faut s'attendre à souffrir* [you must be ready to suffer],' warned Antoine Dubois, one of the most famous surgeons in France and gynaecologist to the Empress Josephine, explaining that removal of the cancer was the only way of saving her life. '*Vous souffrirez beaucoup* [You will suffer greatly].'

Fanny insisted that her husband should not be a witness to the operation, and that she herself should be given only two hours' warning. Had she cried greatly in childbirth? she was asked. Good, came the reply – she should not restrain her screaming when the time came.

At this point the tale becomes gruesome, and the squeamish should read no further. But it stands as a reminder of how countless thousands of men, women and children went bravely under the surgeon's knife in the centuries before the development of anaesthetics in the 1840s. On 30 September 1811 Alexandre d'Arblay was inveigled out of the house on a pretext, and Fanny found herself confronted by seven men in black, the surgeons, plus their pupils and nurses. She saw two old mattresses covered by a sheet and was told to undress and lie down on them. She was given a glass of wine cordial, then blindfolded. She could see the glint of polished steel through the muslin and heard the surgeon ask, '*Qui me tiendra ce sein?* [Who will support the breast?]'

'*C'est moi, monsieur!*' cried out Fanny, holding her own breast – and the surgery began.

My dear Esther [she wrote to her sister], *when the dreadful steel was plunged into the breast – cutting through veins, arteries, flesh, nerves – I needed no injunctions not to restrain my cries. I began a scream that lasted unremittingly during the whole time of the incision – and I almost marvel that it rings not in my ears still, so excruciating was the agony. When the wound was made and the instrument withdrawn, the pain seemed undiminished – but when again I felt the knife, describing a curve, cutting against the grain, if I may say so, then indeed I thought I must have expired.*

As the knife was withdrawn for the second time, Fanny concluded that the operation must be over.

> *Oh no! Presently the terrible cutting was renewed – and worse than ever, to separate the bottom, the foundation of this dreadful gland, from the parts to which it adhered. I felt the knife wrackling against the backbone – scraping it! – I remained in utterly speechless torture.*

Fanny had expected that only the tumour would be cut out. In fact, the seven strong men in black had held her down for a full twenty minutes while her whole breast was removed. But the ghastly pain proved worth while. Fanny Burney was fifty-nine years old at the time of her operation and would survive to the age of eight-eight: she lived twenty-nine years with no recurrence of the cancer.

WHO WAS NED LUDD?

1812

IN 1811 AND 1812 MYSTERIOUS LETTERS STARTED reaching the mill owners of Nottinghamshire and Leicestershire, threatening them with the destruction of their machinery. The threats were sent in the name of Ned Ludd or sometimes General Ludd – and 'the General' proved as good as his word. Well disciplined bands of men began attacking mills and factories after dark in raids of military precision, smashing windows and breaking down doors to destroy the mechanical looms, or 'frames', that were cutting their wages and putting them out of work. It was an organised proliferation of the attacks that had been made in 1766 on James Hargreaves's first spinning jennies.

The attacks soon spread to Lancashire and the West Riding of Yorkshire, where fearful householders listened behind closed shutters to the passing of the General's army – 'a measured, beating, approaching sound, a dull tramp of marching feet,' as Charlotte Brontë described it three decades later, basing her account on those of contemporary newspapers. 'It was not the tread of two, nor of a dozen, nor of a score of men; it was the tread of hundreds.'

'Hundreds' was an underestimate for the size of Ludd's army at its largest. According to the Nottingham correspondent of the *Leeds Mercury*, 'the Insurrectional state to which this county has been reduced . . . has no parallel in history since the troubled days of Charles the First'. At one stage in 1812 there were as many as twelve thousand government troops in the four northern counties trying to hold down the rebellion of the Luddites – a significant drain on the numbers that Britain could deploy in Europe in those years in its epic struggle with Napoleon.

The European war had much to do with the trouble in the factories. Thanks to Trafalgar and the enduring might of the British navy, Napoleon could not invade England. But he had used his control over mainland Europe – and, from 1812, his friendship with America – to wage history's first large-scale economic war, imposing a trade blockade on the British Isles. British merchants and manufacturers found they could not sell their goods. To cut their wage bills, they had to sack workers and make more use of machines. Then a series of bad harvests in the years 1808–12 forced up food prices just when ordinary folk had less money than ever to spend. 'I have five children and a wife,' testified one Manchester worker whose weekly wage was nine old pennies. 'I work sixteen hours a day to get that . . . It will take 2 [pence] per week coals, 1 [penny] per week candles. My family live on potatoes chiefly, and we have one pint of milk per day.'

A number of the disturbances classed as 'Luddite' were, in fact, food riots. In April 1812 police and the army had to intervene in Manchester when desperate women started taking the stock of dealers who were charging fifteen shillings (180 old pence, or twenty weeks' wages) for a load of potatoes.

'Nothing but absolute want could have driven a large and once honest and industrious body of people into the commission of excesses so hazardous to themselves, their family and their community,' protested Lord Byron, speaking in the House of Lords.

The poet was opposing the Frame-Breaking Bill of 1812 by which the government of the day, led by Spencer Perceval, made the destruction of machinery punishable by death. When Perceval himself was murdered a few months later in the lobby of the House of Commons – the only British Prime Minister ever to be assassinated – suspicion fell immediately upon the Luddites. In fact, the killer was a deranged businessman who had been ruined by the collapse of foreign trade.

The original Lud was a mythical king of Britain who was said to have built the first walls of London – Ludgate Hill is named after him. Lud may also have been the name of a Celtic river god, and this name links, in spirit at least, with the machine-breakers of 1811 and 1812, who rallied and drilled their forces in the woods. Some of the letters from 'General Ludd and his Army of Redressers' gave their address as

Sherwood Forest, the home of Robin Hood, who was certainly not a real person but whose legend embodied deeply cherished values to those who felt oppressed.

The Luddites were fighting to protect a centuries-old, craft-based way of life that gave them livelihood and self-respect – and also enshrined a certain commitment to quality. Some of the most savage machine-smashings were directed at the new 'stocking frames', which mass-produced socks by crudely closing and stitching tubes of fabric. Nowadays questions of wages and job security can be approached through negotiation, but there was no collective bargaining in the early nineteenth century. Trades unions were illegal. 'Combinations' of workmen were prohibited by law* – so where else could reformers turn but to the General in the woods? As the authorities clamped down on the Luddites – several dozen were hanged or transported to penal servitude in Australia – the movement was forcibly suppressed.

Today the word 'Luddite' is an insult directed at someone who is thought to be mindlessly blocking progress, particularly technological progress. But were the original Luddites being so mindless when they challenged the tyranny of progress for progress's sake? Quality of life, tradition, social

---

*'An Act to Prevent Unlawful Combinations of Workmen' was passed in 1799, and was reaffirmed and supplemented by a second Combination Act the following year. Prompted by government fears of unrest and that revolution might spread from across the Channel, the combination laws drove trades union activity underground until their repeal in 1824–5. Even then fresh legislation undermined the workers' power to bargain collectively: they had to operate on the fringes of the law until 1860.

justice – in our own age that bows so slavishly to the soulless commands of technology and the marketplace, we might reflect on the protest of General Ludd and keep our ears pricked for his tramp, tramp, tramp in the night.

WELLINGTON AND WATERLOO

1815

IN THE SPRING OF 1793 ARTHUR WESLEY, A 23-year-old army officer who loved playing the violin, proposed to Kitty Pakenham, a dark-haired beauty three years his junior, who lived a day's ride from Dangan, the Wesley home in County Meath. The couple had known each other for several years and, as two young Anglo-Irish aristocrats, they seemed a well suited pair. But Tom, Kitty's elder brother, vetoed the match – the Wesleys were impoverished, and Arthur's army career was going nowhere.

The rejection devastated Arthur Wesley. He burned his violin and never played music again. Resolving to make himself a better officer, he started attending parade-ground drill sessions and applied for active military service abroad. A dozen years later he returned from India with the rank of major general, a knighthood and a fortune of £42,000 that was more than enough to keep Kitty Pakenham in style. The couple married in Dublin in April 1806.

It would be nice to report that the Wellesleys (Arthur changed the spelling of his surname in 1798) lived happily ever after. In fact, Arthur started repenting at the altar – 'She has grown ugly, by Jove!' he confided to his brother Gerald – and his marriage proved one of the least happy aspects of his glittering career. Kitty, for her part, soon gave up the impossible task of pleasing her demanding husband, who treated her like a child. 'She is like the housekeeper and dresses herself exactly like a shepherdess,' sneered one of Arthur's glossy lady friends, 'with an old hat made by herself stuck on the back of her head, and a dirty basket under her arm.' The couple had two sons together, but little happiness.

Arthur Wellesley was to win his famous title, Duke of Wellington, for the brave and dogged military campaigns he fought against the French forces occupying Spain and Portugal – the Peninsular War that marked the turning-point in the struggle against Napoleon. In August 1808 he landed north of Lisbon with the first detachment of just nine thousand British troops, sent to assist the popular revolt against the French Emperor's placing of his brother Joseph Bonaparte on the throne of Spain. In the next six years he retrained the Portuguese army, collaborated with the Spanish guerrillas, and welded his own, often outnumbered, forces into a grimly efficient fighting machine.

Wellington was as sternly disciplined with his soldiers as

he was with himself – among his many innovations was a new system of military police. But his men were devoted to 'Atty' (for Arthur) or 'Nosey', as they called their hardworking general, who rose every morning at six and spent the day busying himself with every little detail of his army's welfare.

After fighting from the Atlantic to the Pyrenees, the British army invaded southwestern France in the spring of 1814, to hear that Napoleon, broken by his Russian campaign and finally defeated at the Battle of Leipzig, had abdicated. Wellington marched into Paris in triumph, but as someone disobligingly reminded him, all his peninsular victories had been won against Napoleon's marshals – he had never been compelled to face the French Emperor in battle.

'I am very glad I never was,' replied the Duke candidly. 'I would at any time rather have heard that a reinforcement of 40,000 men had joined the French army, than that he had arrived to take command.'

'Nosey' versus 'Boney' seemed a fanciful historical might-have-been as Wellington travelled to Vienna to join the victorious allies in the remaking of Europe, while Napoleon languished in exile on the island of Elba. But on 7 March 1815, as Wellington was pulling on his boots for his favourite relaxation, a ride to hounds, came the astonishing news that Bonaparte had escaped. The ex-Emperor had landed in the south of France with just a handful of men, and as he marched north towards Paris, the whole country turned to him.

Wellington faced a formidable task as he set about organising the allied armies with their different languages, training, experience and weaponry. He had to share responsibility for the defence of the Netherlands with the venerable

Prussian general, Blücher, and he could get no reliable intelligence about his enemy's plans. 'I had never seen him have such an expression of care and anxiety upon his countenance,' recorded Lady Hamilton-Dalrymple as she sat beside Wellington at the Duchess of Richmond's ball, held in Brussels on 15 June that year.

'Napoleon has humbugged me, by God,' the Duke exclaimed as he received news, some time after midnight, that the French army was heading straight for Brussels. 'He has gained twenty-four hours' march on me.'

Calling for a map, he traced the position of the troops he had deployed to defend the city, and placed his thumb on a ridge to the southwest – 'I must fight him here.' His thumb was on a hamlet called Waterloo.

Wellington later described the battle as a 'pounding match'. Napoleon had never before encountered the obstinate skill with which the Duke had learned in the Peninsula to keep defending a fortified position, and the French wore themselves out attacking the disciplined blocks of British and allied troops. When Blücher arrived towards the end of the day, his Prussian soldiers tipped the balance. The French army broke and fled.

Waterloo confirmed Wellington's place as one of Britain's greatest ever military leaders, and he went on to a controversial career in politics, serving as Prime Minister from 1828 to 1830 – the windows of his home at Hyde Park Corner, Apsley House,* were smashed twice by angry mobs, enraged

---

*Known as 'Number One, London' because it was the first house you met as you entered London through the tollgate.

by his anti-libertarian views and policies. But the 'Iron Duke' would go quiet whenever Waterloo was mentioned, remembering the victims – some 17,000 British, 7000 Prussians and 26,000 French – whose lives were the price of victory. 'It is a bad thing to be always fighting,' he said. 'It is quite impossible to think of glory. Both mind and feelings are exhausted. I am wretched at the moment of victory . . . Next to a battle lost, the greatest misery is a battle gained.'

STONE TREASURES – MARY ANNING AND THE TERROR LIZARDS

1823

THE SOFT AND FOSSIL-RICH LIMESTONE CLIFFS of Lyme Regis on the border of Devon and Dorset are forever crumbling – it is as if the earth's crust has been turned inside out – and from an early age Mary Anning loved to walk with her dog among the debris, chipping out stone treasures with a little hammer and pickaxe that she carried, together with a basket. The Anning family eked out a living in the early years of the nineteenth century selling these 'snake stones' and 'verteberries' to visitors – they had a tiny tumbledown shop beside the beach. But Mary was much more than a beachcomber.

'The extraordinary thing about this young woman,' wrote one visitor in the 1820s, 'is that she has made herself so thoroughly acquainted with the science that the moment she finds any bones she knows to what tribe they belong. She fixes the bones on a frame with cement and then makes drawings and has them engraved.'

The twin disciplines of geology (the study of the earth), and palaeontology (the study of 'early things') were just developing, and as the experts heard of Mary's work they hurried down from their universities and learned societies to Lyme Regis. 'By reading and application,' wrote Lady Harriet Silvester, 'she has arrived to that degree of knowledge as to be in the habit of writing and talking with professors and other clever men on the subject and they all acknowledge that she understands more of the science than anyone else in this kingdom.'

If Mary Anning ever alighted on an especially large treasure, she would go for help, leaving her dog to guard the spot, and in December 1823 she needed a large digging party to unearth the fossilised bones of a nine-foot monster that seemed to be a cross between a turtle and a snake. Its spine alone comprised ninety 'verteberries', with fourteen ribs and three surviving fine-boned paddles instead of feet. Academics identified the discovery as the world's first ever complete example of a 'plesiosaur' – a 'near-lizard'.

Modern science sets the plesiosaurs in the Mesozoic era, living 245 to 65 million years ago in that distantly frightening period that most people today accept as 'prehistoric'. But in 1823 many preachers taught their congregations that God had made the world less than six thousand years previously, even fixing on a precise date – 4004 BC. According to the Book of Genesis, the whole of Creation was accomplished in just six days. How could a loving God have filled the earth with these sinister creeping things?* And how did the age of lizards fit in with the story of the Flood – or with Adam and Eve, for that matter? The Bible did not even mention the giant reptiles' existence.

Mary was a devout chapel-goer, but these questions did not trouble her. The little bonneted figure could frequently be seen scouring the Dorset cliffs, making her discoveries – among them some of the earliest and finest examples of ichthyosaurs (fish lizards), and the first British 'flying dragon', the pterodactyl (so named from the Greek *pteron*, wing, and *daktulos*, finger). By the time of her death in 1847 Mary had become the heroine of England's Jurassic coast, awarded annuities by Parliament, by the Geological Society and by the British Association for the Advancement of Science. But she would have traded them all for her name at the top of a learned article. As she remarked one day to a young woman with whom she went out fossilling, 'these men of learning have made a great deal by publishing works of which I furnished the contents'. They had 'sucked my brains,' said Mary – and then quietly resumed her chipping.

---

*The word 'dinosaur', coined in 1842, means 'terrible' or 'fearfully great' lizard.

BLOOD ON THE TRACKS

1830

RAIN WAS FALLING GENTLY ON THE
morning of 15 September 1830, as crowds gathered in
Lancashire to ogle an array of locomotive engines. Until
quite recently all 'engines' had been stationary pieces of
machinery – solidly fixed in one place. But the newly developed locomotive engines had the power to shift themselves
(from the Latin words *loco*, to or from a place, and *motivus*,
moving), and now, to mark the opening of this freshly built
stretch of railway line running thirty-three miles between
the growing connurbations of Liverpool and Manchester, the
new locomotives were demonstrating how they could reliably
transport both goods and people.

Pride of place went to the stubby and muscular-looking *Rocket*, a formidable assemblage of brass, iron and steel that had been bolted together by the father-and-son team of George and Robert Stephenson. With steam oozing from her twin pistons, angled on either side of her boiler like the haunches of some gigantic frog ready to leap forward along the track, the *Rocket* embodied all the power and menace that frightened people about the railways: birds would be killed by the smoke, warned the doom-mongers, and cows' milk would curdle as the noisy trains sped past; it was even suggested that passengers' lungs would collapse under the pressure of high speeds. On the other side of the Pennines, the Duke of Cleveland had held up the Stockton and Darlington line for three years for fear of what it would do to his foxes.

The *Mechanic's Magazine* for September 1830 sought to allay such fears. 'We think we shall not go too far in saying that [the new invention] will produce an entire change in the face of British society,' the journal told its readers, predicting the growth of what would become known as the suburb and the stockbroker belt. 'Living in the country will no longer be a term synonymous with every sort of inconvenience, and it will come to be a mere matter of choice whether a man of business works close by his country house or thirty miles from it.'

One particular advocate of the railways was the MP for Liverpool, William Huskisson, who had served as President of the Board of Trade in 1823. Huskisson had proved himself quite a reformer, cutting trade tariffs and angering many employers by arguing for the repeal of the Combination Acts so that workers could organise trades unions. Some of his wealthiest supporters owned shares in the local canals, whose transport business would be drastically undercut by the speed and economy of the new railway line between Liverpool and Manchester; but that did not stop Huskisson working hard to get the line approved by Parliament. It would benefit all classes of the local workforce, he told the Liverpool newspapers, and he prepared a speech to deliver on the evening of 15 September at the dinner that had been arranged to celebrate the grand opening of the line.

'The principle of a Railway is that of commerce itself,' he planned to say. 'It multiplies the enjoyment of Mankind by increasing the facilities and diminishing the labour by which the means of those enjoyments are produced and distributed throughout the world.'

William Huskisson never got to deliver his speech. The guest of honour at the railway opening was none other than the Duke of Wellington, who had been Prime Minister since January, and Huskisson travelled in one of the carriages that set off with the Duke and other VIPs eastwards from Liverpool at eleven o'clock that morning. Just before noon, after travelling nearly eighteen miles – halfway to Manchester – the convoy of carriages stopped at Parkside Station, and Huskisson got out to join the crowd milling around Wellington's carriage.

Suddenly a shout went up – 'An engine is approaching. Take care, gentlemen!' It was the *Rocket*, careering along the northern track in the opposite direction, from Manchester. 'You had better step in!' the Duke called down from his carriage to Huskisson, who was standing on the gravel between the two tracks. Most people had dashed for the embankment, but after havering to and fro, Huskisson chose to cling on to the carriage. There was a gap of just over four feet (1.25 metres) between the two lines, and the MP would have been safe if he had stayed in place. But losing his nerve, he made a grab for the door of the Duke's carriage, which swung open with his weight – right into the path of the advancing *Rocket*.

Flung down on to the track, Huskisson suffered ghastly injuries – the wheels of the locomotive passed over his left leg, crushing bone and muscle and spraying out blood, to the horror of the spectators. As the MP was rushed away for medical attention, the Duke reluctantly agreed to continue the ride to Manchester. But the celebratory dinner that night was a subdued affair, the tone set by a mournful toast to William Huskisson – 'May his sufferings be speedily assuaged, and his health restored.' By 11 p.m., in fact, when the toast was delivered, the local champion of the railway had already died, his agonies only partially relieved by heavy doses of laudanum (opium in alcohol).

Fifty thousand mourners attended the funeral of William Huskisson. Liverpool closed down for the day. But that did not deter people from using the railway. In its very first week the new line carried 6104 fare-paying passengers, and within twelve months that figure had risen to nearly half a million. Most of these were pulled by the *Rocket*, now beloved as a pioneer of locomotive transportation, fully justifying Huskisson's prophecies. But he would be remembered as a pioneer of another sort – the first passenger fatality in the age of high-speed mechanical travel.

THE LUNG POWER OF
ORATOR HUNT

1819–32

HENRY 'ORATOR' HUNT OWED HIS NICKNAME to his prodigious lung capacity – he could project his voice like a trumpet. Such decibel power was precious to a public speaker in an age before microphones – and to make quite sure that the furthest member of his audience could also see him, the barrel-chested Hunt would complete the picture with a large white top-hat.

One sultry day in August 1819, Orator Hunt rose to bellow out his message to a crowd of some sixty thousand men, women and children who had gathered in St Peter's Fields, Manchester. They were working people mostly, rallying in the cause of parliamentary reform and the right of all men to vote by secret ballot. But Hunt had not got ten minutes into his speech when a party of blue-and-white-clad cavalrymen came clip-clopping round the corner, their drawn swords raised in front of them.

The meeting had been quiet until that point, and the crowd greeted the soldiers with a shout of goodwill. But the cavalry's response was to ride their horses fiercely into the rally. 'Their sabres were plied to hew a way through naked held-up hands and defenceless heads,' wrote one eyewitness. 'Women, white-vested maids and tender youths were indiscriminately sabred or trampled.'

Within ten minutes the soldiery had cleared St Peter's Fields of people, as they had been ordered to do by local magistrates, leaving at least eleven people dead and more than five hundred wounded in what became known – in a derisive reference to the recent British victory at Waterloo – as the 'Peterloo' Massacre. The Cheshire magistrates had hoped to silence Hunt by ordering his arrest, but instead they turned him into a national celebrity. More than three hundred thousand people cheered the orator through the streets on the way to one of his trials, and when he started writing from his prison cell his memoirs became a serial bestseller (in forty-six instalments) – dedicated 'To the Radical Reformers, Male and Female, of England, Ireland and Scotland'.

At first glance, Hunt seems an unlikely candidate for radical martyrdom. His ancestors were Norman, his great-great-grandfather was a loyalist who went into exile with Charles II, and he himself farmed three thousand acres (over 1200 hectares) on which he produced fine grains and employed

GREAT TALES FROM ENGLISH HISTORY

the latest sheep-farming techniques. But when, following the failure of his marriage, he took up with the unhappy wife of a friend, he found himself shunned by 'polite' society. He reacted with prickliness – rows with the commanding officer of the local yeomanry and with his neighbours landed him in jail in 1800 and again in 1810 – and he developed a hatred of the landed upper classes who dominated nineteenth-century British life.

Their domination was most powerfully expressed through the rickety parliamentary system that dated back to medieval times. Ancient and decayed communities retained the right to send MPs to Westminster – the seven voters of Old Sarum in Wiltshire, for instance, returned two MPs to Parliament. Many of these 'rotten' or 'pocket' boroughs were in the south, while the new industrial communities of the Midlands and the north were under-represented: Manchester, Birmingham, Leeds and Sheffield had no MPs at all. Of the nearly four-teen million people living in England and Wales in 1831, only four hundred thousand or so had the vote: all these voters were men, and they had to step up on to the hustings to cast their vote in public.

Orator Hunt called for universal male suffrage by secret ballot – as people vote today. So long as men had to declare their allegiance publicly, he argued, they would feel com-pelled to toe the line of their bosses and landlords. At the end of the eighteenth century the Earl of Lonsdale con-trolled no fewer than nine constituencies on his various estates – his MPs were known as his 'ninepins': by one esti-mate, just 87 peers controlled 213 of the Commons' 658 seats.

By 1830 the stentorian trumpet of Orator Hunt was one of many voices calling for change. That autumn discontented labourers in Kent, Sussex, Hampshire and Berkshire responded to the call of a mythical 'Captain Swing' – a southern version of General Ludd – to set fire to the harvest and to smash their masters' threshing machines. The hayricks were burning as Parliament assembled, creating a mood that swept aside the Duke of Wellington and his Tory government.

His replacement, the elegant and elderly Lord Grey, was no radical – he oversaw the rounding-up of two thousand 'Captain Swing' rioters, 19 of whom were executed, 481 transported, and 644 sent to prison. But Grey understood the need for concession. 'The principle of my reform is to prevent the necessity for revolution,' he told Parliament; '. . . reforming to preserve, not to overthrow.' Doggedly fighting and negotiating for more than a year, Grey finally saw his Reform Bill into law on 4 June 1832, abolishing the 'rotten' boroughs and doubling the size of the electorate by extending the vote to a variety of small property-holders.

Orator Hunt participated vigorously in the epic battle over Reform. He got himself elected as the MP for Preston in Lancashire and made no less than a thousand speeches *against* Grey's proposals, which he saw as a betrayal of 'the unrepresented seven millions of working men in England'. Reform was a trick, he complained, to get 'the middle classes, the little shopkeepers and those people, to join the higher classes'.

His argument had merit: 1832 marked the end of the old system – it was a genuine, hard-fought turning-point in which Hunt himself had played his part. But the expanded new electorate of 814,000 was still only one in five males – and without a secret ballot it was as vulnerable as ever to the arm-twisting of landlords and bosses, who would remain the masters of political Britain for decades to come.

Orator Hunt died in 1835, dispirited and poverty-stricken, but battling to the end. One of his projects, to rebuild the fortune that he lost in his political campaigning, was 'Hunt's Matchless Shoe-Blacking'. It promised your shoes a perfect shine, and on every bottle was embossed the legend: 'Equal Laws. Equal Rights. Annual Parliaments, Universal Suffrage and the Ballot.'

THE TOLPUDDLE MARTYRS

1834

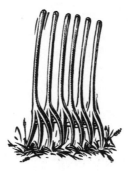

PLOUGHMEN, LABOURERS, SHEPHERDS, COW-herds, pigmen, hedgers, thatchers, dairymen, black-smiths, gamekeepers – for much of the nineteenth century the largest single group of British workers were the men who worked on the land, and often they were poorly paid. Ten shillings (50p) per week was considered the minimum on which a family could survive in the 1830s, but in the village of Tolpuddle in Dorset the day came when the farm labourers found themselves expected to make do on nine.

'After some months we were reduced to eight shillings,' related George Loveless, a labourer who also preached in the local Methodist chapels. 'This caused great dissatisfaction, and all the labouring men in the village, with the exception of two or three invalids, made application [for Poor Relief] to a neighbouring magistrate.'

There were just six able-bodied men living in Tolpuddle, whose picturesque name was of Anglo-Saxon origin, meaning marshy, low-lying land, probably belonging to a widow called Tola* – and they received short shrift from the bench. 'We were told that we must work for whatever our employers thought fit to give us, as there was no law to compel masters to give any fixed sum of money to their servants.' And there was worse to come – their wages were soon reduced to seven shillings, with the threat that six was not far behind.

In desperation, the Tolpuddle Six decided to form a Friendly Society of Agricultural Labourers to campaign for better wages – only to find themselves arrested on 24 February 1834 and marched in chains to the county town of Dorchester, where they were charged with taking part in an initiation ceremony at which illegal oaths had been administered.

The charge was an obscure one, deriving from a statute designed to punish naval mutiny. Moderate wage campaigning had been legal since the repeal of the Combination Acts in 1824. But the Dorset authorities, like the Manchester magistrates who ordered troops to arrest Orator Hunt in St Peter's Fields, were determined to crack down on what they

---

*Tola owned the land in 1050. Nearby villages on the River Piddle (a variant of Puddle) included Affpuddle, almost certainly named after Alfridus who was the landowner in 987.

viewed as revolutionary activity. At the Dorchester Assizes in March 1834, George Loveless and his five fellow labourers from Tolpuddle were found guilty, and dispatched to serve seven years in Australia as convict labourers.

The outcry was immediate. Twenty-five thousand workers marched through the streets of London in one of the largest peaceful demonstrations ever seen in the capital. 'Arise, men of Britain and take your stand!' exhorted the London–Dorchester Labourers' Committee. 'Rally round the standard of liberty! Or for ever lay prostrate under the hand of your land- and money-mongering taskmasters!' Within a year the Home Secretary Lord John Russell had granted the men conditional pardons. In 1836 the pardons became full, and in 1837 the six started coming home to a succession of celebratory processions and dinners, which most of them – modest souls – found deeply embarrassing.

The 'martyrs' had become symbols. The flagrant injustice of their deportation, coupled with the men's own meekness – and also, perhaps, the comical name of their little village – helped stimulate working-class consciousness. The year 1839 saw the beginnings of the Chartist movement, dedicated to securing a charter of reforms that included the right to vote of *all* adult males, not just property-holders, and a call for the introduction of the secret ballot. Chartist demonstrations and ongoing radical pressure would eventually result in the Second Reform Act of 1867, which considerably extended the franchise, along with the Ballot Act of 1872 which finally realised Orator Hunt's dream of the secret vote.

But by 1872 only one of the six martyrs was still living in Tolpuddle. The others had emigrated to Canada. Having been transported once against their will, they now transported themselves voluntarily, though they never gave the reason why, and they carefully hid their Tolpuddle identities from their new friends and neighbours. The famous five did not even tell their Canadian-born children about their past – they wanted to escape from all of that. There was more to life than being a symbol.

'I WILL BE GOOD' – VICTORIA
BECOMES QUEEN

1837

PREPARING ONE DAY IN 1830 FOR A HISTORY lesson in her solitary schoolroom at Kensington Palace, the eleven-year-old Princess Victoria opened her exercise book to be confronted by a family tree. Her governess had put it there for her to study. The table of descent explained the relationships inside the House of Hanover – Victoria's own family – and as the Princess started tracing her personal connection with her grandfather King George III, she worked out something that had been concealed from her until that point in her life.

'I see I am nearer the throne than I thought,' she said – in fact, she was almost certain to become Queen. As the impact of this awe-inspiring prospect sank in, the little girl burst into tears. Yet even in her most emotional moments there was always a part of Victoria that remained detached: 'I will be good,' she said.

The family table showed that, by 1819, George III's seven surviving adult sons had, astonishingly, failed to produce a single legitimate living heir between them. The men – most of them portly, all of them spoilt, and all degenerate or defective in different, ingenious ways – had fathered bastards aplenty. Their mistresses and messy love lives had prompted scandal and widespread contempt for the royal family. Only with the birth of Victoria in May 1819 had the direct succession become reasonably safe – though the sudden death of her father Edward, Duke of Kent (the old King's fourth son), eight months later, demonstrated the perils of becoming ill in an age of poor health care. He had caught a chill at the seaside.

Victoria's mother, the widowed Duchess, was determined to keep her daughter safe and close to her in every way. The girl was not allowed to go downstairs without holding someone's hand. She had to sleep in the same bedroom as her mother, and she was shielded from 'unsuitable' personal influences by a cocoon of rules and protocol known as the 'Kensington System'. The Princess scarcely ever met children of her own age – for amusement and simple affection her solitary playmate was her beloved dog Dash, a King Charles spaniel.

Critics suspected that the main purpose of the Kensington System was to secure the position of Sir John Conroy, a handsome but slippery Irish adventurer who had become the confidant of the Duchess – and sure enough, when Victoria fell seriously ill on a visit to Ramsgate in 1835, Conroy tried to force the weakened Princess to sign a document that would make him her private secretary when she became Queen. The Duchess joined in, with a crude mix of threats and emotional blackmail, but the ailing sixteen-year-old withstood their pressure.

Two years later, in the quiet dawn hours of 20 June 1837, the Lord Chamberlain and the Archbishop of Canterbury came hurrying through the trees to knock on the door of Kensington Palace. Roused from her sleep, the eighteen-year-old Victoria received them in her dressing-gown – to see the venerable old gentlemen fall on their knees in front of her. Her uncle William IV had died in the night, and she was now Queen.

That night, for the first time in her life, Victoria slept on her own. She ordered her things to be moved to her own quarters – and in the weeks that followed she firmly detached herself from her mother. When the Duchess sent requests to see her daughter she would often receive notes containing just one word, 'Busy'. Sir John Conroy was forbidden access to the new Queen's apartments at Buckingham Palace.

Victoria was displaying all the fortitude that would characterise her sixty-three years on the throne – the longest reign to date in the history of the British monarchy. The adjective 'Victorian', meaning stern and dutiful, derived directly from her character. But the little Queen (she was less than five feet tall) had a playful and deeply sentimental side. When she got back to Buckingham Palace on 28 June 1838 at the end of her solemn and arduous coronation ceremonies, Her Majesty rushed straight upstairs to give a bath to her best friend Dash.

'GOD'S WONDERFUL RAILWAY' –
ISAMBARD KINGDOM BRUNEL

1843

ONE DAY IN 1843, ISAMBARD KINGDOM
Brunel was entertaining some children with his favourite party trick. Brandishing a half-sovereign, the Victorian equivalent of a 50p piece, the ingenious engineer would make the coin appear to vanish down his throat, then pluck it dramatically from his ear. Unfortunately for Brunel, on this occasion he really did swallow the coin – it slipped down his throat to become lodged in his windpipe.

For weeks the famous maker of railways, bridges, tunnels, docks and ships coughed painfully. A distinguished surgeon cut a hole in the windpipe and fumbled his forceps inside – to no avail. So the engineer decided to adopt an engineering solution. He designed a rotating table to which he could be strapped, face down. The table was then upended, with Brunel's head pointing towards the floor. With gravity thus enlisted, and the help of some hearty back-slapping, the coin came tumbling out.

Newspapers had been following the saga with horrified fascination – *The Times* ran daily bulletins on Brunel's health – and the reappearance of the coin was a national event. 'It's out! It's out!' cried the great historian Thomas Macaulay as he went running down the street. Everybody knew what he meant.

Brunel had been making headlines since 1826 when, aged only twenty, he took over the ambitious project started by his father, the French engineer Marc Brunel, to build a tunnel under the Thames from Rotherhithe to Wapping in London's docklands – the world's first underwater walkway. Isambard ('Kingdom' was the surname of his English mother Sophia) nearly died when the river broke through the tunnel roof and swept him away; but the young man survived to repair the tunnel and stage a spectacular candle-lit dinner for the project's directors below the riverbed. Brunel understood how visionary engineering needed show-manship to sell it, and he made himself a celebrity in the process.

The merchants of Bristol decided to enlist his flair. They were planning a 'Great Western Railway' to link the port with London, and the 27-year-old took on the project, exploring on horseback the 110 miles of countryside between London and Bristol to plot out the route with the gentlest, and thus the speediest, gradients. This involved some tunnelling again – Brunel's two-mile-long tunnel at Box, west of Swindon, took almost six years to complete, and when the crews digging from each end met in the middle, in 1840, they were found to be only one and a quarter inches out of alignment. Over the Thames at Maidenhead, Brunel constructed an elegant, flat-arched bridge whose spans were so level they seemed to be held up by magic. To this day they remain the widest, flat, brick-built arches in the world.

With its engineering marvels and soaring cathedral-like stations (also designed by Brunel), the GWR became nick-named 'God's Wonderful Railway'. In 1842 Queen Victoria chose the GWR for her first trip by train – and by that date the railway had an extra dimension. 'Why not make it longer and have a steamboat go from Bristol to New York?' Brunel had suggested when one GWR director expressed worries about the length of the track. So in 1837 he had launched the *Great Western*, a huge paddle-steamer that carried passengers across the Atlantic in fifteen days and managed the return voyage in one day less. In the spring of 1843 (at the same time that he was trying to extricate the half-sovereign from his throat) he launched an even larger vessel, the *Great Britain*, the first iron-hulled, screw-propeller-driven ship the world had ever seen.

But the *Great Britain* lost money for its investors. Fare-paying passengers seemed wary of the ship's gargantuan bulk, and their fears were realised when, after only three trans-atlantic return voyages, she ran aground on the coast of Ireland. Not for the first time, Brunel's visionary ambition outran the practicalities. Extending the GWR into Devon, he built an 'atmospheric railway' that did away with noisy, soot-showering locomotives. Connected by iron rods to a vacuum tube between the rails, the carriages were sucked along by the vacuum inside the tube that was created and maintained by pumping-stations along the track.

But Brunel's system depended on the air-tightness of a leather flap along the top of the tube. This opened and closed to allow the passage of the iron rod below each carriage, and its suppleness was maintained by men who patrolled the line, painting the leather with a mixture of lime soap and whale oil. Unfortunately the taste of the whale oil was immensely appealing to rats, and as the rodents tucked into the oily leather, the atmospheric railway kept losing its atmospheric pressure.

Brunel took responsibility for the failure of his bold experiment – and he died in the middle of another, the launching in 1859 of his monster of monsters the *Great Eastern*, a 692-foot (210-metre) paddle-steamer that displaced 28,000 tons, five times more than any ship then afloat. Designed to carry four thousand, the *Great Eastern* carried just thirty-six passengers on her maiden voyage and ended her days as a cable-laying ship.

Brunel was only fifty-three when he died, but he had crammed several lifetimes into one. Nowadays he would be called a workaholic. He laboured every day and most of the night in a cloud of tobacco smoke, chain-smoking cigars. He drove his workforce fiercely – a hundred men were killed hacking through the solid rock of Box Tunnel – and he was as hard on his family as he was on himself.

By the time of his death, the commercial world had come

to view him as dangerously extravagant – and so he was, agreed Daniel Gooch, the friend and colleague who built his locomotives for the GWR. But, added Gooch, 'great things are not done by those who count the cost of every thought and act'.

RAIN, STEAM & SPEED – THE SHIMMERING VISION OF J.M.W. TURNER

1843

ONE JUNE EVENING IN 1843 A YOUNG woman, Jane O'Meara, was travelling to London on the recently constructed Great Western Railway through a terrifying storm. Thunder roared and lightning flashed across the countryside, while torrents of sheeting rain attacked the windows – so Jane was surprised when one of the elderly gentlemen travelling in her First Class carriage asked if she would mind him putting the rain-blurred window down. He wanted to take a look outside.

Politely consenting, Jane was still more surprised when

her travelling companion thrust his head and shoulders out into the storm and kept them resolutely there for nearly nine minutes. The old man was evidently engrossed by what he saw, and when he finally drew back in, drenched, the young woman could not resist the temptation to put her own head out of the window – to be astonished by a blurred cacophony of sound and brightness. The train was standing at that moment in Bristol Temple Meads Station, and the mingled impression of steam, sulphurous smoke and the flickering glow from the engine's firebox overwhelmed her – 'such a chaos of elemental and artificial lights and noises,' she later wrote, 'I never saw or heard, or expect to see or hear.'

Almost a year later, going to look at the new pictures being hung in that summer's Royal Academy exhibition, Jane O'Meara suddenly realised who the eccentric traveller must have been. For hanging on the gallery wall, depicted in swirling and unconventional swathes of paint, was the same scary yet compelling vortex of light and turbulence that she had seen from her GWR carriage window – *Rain, Steam & Speed* by J.M.W. Turner.

By 1844 Joseph Mallord William Turner was a renowned, controversial and highly successful artist. He was born sixty-nine years earlier to a poor barber-wigmaker near London's Covent Garden fruit and vegetable market, and a mentally fragile mother who ended her days in the Bethlehem hospital for lunatics – 'Bedlam'. Turner retained his gruff Cockney accent all his life, along with a shrewd commercial spirit that dated back to the days when he exhibited his first paintings in his father's shop window at one shilling (5p) each.

Turner's wild, tumultuous and almost abstract paintings

were denounced as 'mad' by many Victorians. But the French painters Monet, Renoir, Pissarro and Degas would later pay tribute to the 'the illustrious Turner' as the artist whose interest in 'the fugitive effects of light' inspired their own great revolution in ways of seeing – Impressionism. Monet came to London as a young artist to study *Rain, Steam & Speed* which, from the moment of its first hanging in the Royal Academy, was acknowledged by both its admirers and its detractors to be an extraordinary creation. 'The world has never seen anything like this picture,' declared the novelist William Thackeray.

The central feature of the picture was the glowing 'chaos' of light and energy that had shocked Jane O'Meara in Temple Meads Station – transposed by Turner to Brunel's famous bridge at Maidenhead in the Thames Valley, one of the artist's favourite locales for sketching. Enveloped in smoke and mist, the dark and sinister funnel of the locomotive is dashing forwards out of the canvas, a black stovepipe cutting ferociously through the slanting rain, while in front of the careering train – only visible if you step up to the canvas and peer closely – runs a terrified little brown hare, the creature that used to symbolise speed in the age before machines.

Rain, Steam & Speed now hangs in the National Gallery in London's Trafalgar Square. Standing back from its foaming confusion of colours and textures, you cannot help but be struck by the majesty of the world's first great railway painting. You can also recapture the excitement of Jane O'Meara, putting her head out into the storm to see what had caught the visionary eye of Joseph Mallord William Turner.

PRINCE ALBERT'S
CRYSTAL PALACE

1851

O N 1 MAY 1851 QUEEN VICTORIA, DRESSED in a pink crinoline that sparkled with jewels and silver embroidery, clip-clopped in her carriage to Hyde Park to open the largest greenhouse the world had ever seen. Extending over nineteen acres and nicknamed the 'Crystal Palace', the soaring steel structure contained 294,000 panes of glass and was tall enough to accommodate the park's towering old elm trees – along with a hundred thousand extraordinary objects gathered from Britain, Europe, America, Australia, India and China: 'The Great Exhibition of the Works of Industry of All Nations'.

The Great Exhibition was the work of Victoria's husband,

Prince Albert of Saxe-Coburg-Gotha. Victoria had not been impressed when the two first met as teenagers – the solemn young German had nodded off to sleep when the time came to start dancing. But he had learned to dance by the time they met again, on 10 October 1839. 'It is quite a pleasure to look at Albert when he galops and valses,' noted the young Queen appreciatively in her diary. 'My heart is quite going.'

Five days later *she* proposed to *him* (protocol forbade the other way round), and the couple embarked on a passionate marriage that produced nine children – Britain had her first sentimental 'royal family'. Paintings and the recently invented photographic camera showed the royal clan playing with dogs, enjoying country holidays and singing carols round the Christmas tree – a German tradition that Britain now adopted enthusiastically. When it came to politics, Albert understood the importance of royal neutrality, trying to moderate his wife's fierce likings and dislikings for her successive prime ministers; he also appreciated the role the monarchy could play in raising the national spirit.

This was why he encouraged the idea of the Great Exhibition when it was put to him – and the show's popularity went on to justify his faith. More than six million people, a quarter of the country's entire population, flocked to Hyde Park to inspect the wonders of the Crystal Palace in the six months it was open – Queen Victoria herself visited no less than thirty-four times. Among the exhibits were the massive Koh-i-noor diamond, the world's largest mirror which ran the full length of the Palace's Main Avenue, and an 'alarm bed' that tipped over to eject the sleeper out and on to the floor. The serried ranks of public conveniences erected by

George Jennings, the sanitary engineer, were a much discussed novelty, operated by coin-in-the-slot locks that would give rise to the expression 'spend a penny'.

Queen Victoria was struck by a machine that manufactured envelopes – it folded the paper as if it had fingers – and there were more glimpses of the world's mechanical future on the American stands, which displayed the first typewriter and sewing machine along with the mechanical harvesters and threshers that were transforming the power and prosperity of the young United States.

'Dearest Albert's name is for ever immortalised,' wrote Victoria with satisfaction on the day the exhibition opened, and that proved even more the case after it had closed. The show made a handsome surplus, which funded a dream that the Prince had long been nursing – to build a permanent campus of national culture and learning in South Kensington. Albert would die in 1861, aged only forty-two, diagnosed with typhoid fever, the dirty-water disease that poisoned city life in the years before effective public health regulations. But the profits of his Great Exhibition made it possible for his dream to take shape on a swathe of land running down from Hyde Park – the huge, circular Albert Hall for concerts; Imperial College, Britain's premier institution for the teaching of science; the Science Museum; the Natural History Museum; and the domestic design and arts museum now named after Victoria and Albert.

The Crystal Palace itself was carefully dismantled, girder by girder, pane by pane, and started a new life on Sydenham Hill in south London, where it was rebuilt by its architect Sir Joseph Paxton as the centrepiece of a two-hundred-acre

Victorian theme park – the world's first, featuring huge, life-size models of dinosaurs set in a prehistoric swamp. Later came a rollercoaster, a cricket ground and a football club, Crystal Palace FC, a founder member of the Football Association. From 1895 to 1914 the FA Cup Final was played beside the Crystal Palace, and the glorious glass edifice dominated the south London skyline until November 1936, when it was destroyed in a spectacular fire. The flames lit up the sky as far as Brighton. But the name lives on – and you can still go up Sydenham Hill to see the dinosaurs.

'WOMEN AND CHILDREN FIRST!' – THE BIRKENHEAD DRILL

1852

S TEAMING OFF THE COAST OF SOUTH AFRICA late in February 1852, HM Troopship *Birkenhead*, a paddle-steamer, was one of the first iron-hulled ships built for the Royal Navy. She was carrying British troops, many of them raw recruits, with a small consignment of wives and children, to fight in the Kaffir Wars – an empire-building enterprise to conquer the territory of the Xhosa people in the eastern Cape.*

The sea was calm, the sky bright with stars, and most of

---

*In modern times the liberated Xhosa have provided the first two presidents of democratic South Africa, Nelson Mandela and Thabo Mbeki.

the six hundred or so passengers and crew were sound asleep. Looking over the port rail, the small group of sailors who were manning the watch could make out the distant outline of the shore to the left-hand side of the ship, when, just before 2 a.m., a loud crash brought the *Birkenhead* to a juddering halt. Travelling at 8 knots (nearly 15 kilometres per hour) the vessel had driven hard on to an uncharted rock.

Instantly the lower troop deck was flooded, and as water came pouring through a gash in the *Birkenhead*'s iron cladding dozens of soldiers were drowned in their hammocks. Up on deck the crew struggled to release the lifeboats, to find that most were rusted in their davits. Only three boats could be launched, and the ship's commander, Captain Robert Salmond, ordered that the twenty-plus women and children on board should be dispatched to safety, along with the sick.

Elsewhere on deck, Colonel Alexander Seton of the 74th Highlanders took command of the troops, ordering them to line up in their regimental groupings. Many were boys and young men who had been in uniform only a few weeks, but they quickly assembled in their ten detachments, rank after rank, in parade-ground formation.

Now came the moment that distinguished the sinking of the *Birkenhead* from the sad but not uncommon fate of many ships in the centuries before radar, sonar and satellite weather-forecasting. Seeing that the vessel would not stay afloat much longer – she sank, in fact, within twenty minutes of being holed – Captain Salmond gave the order to swim for the boats, only to be countermanded by his army opposite number, Colonel Seton.

'You will swamp the cutter containing the women and children!' cried the colonel. 'I implore you not to do this thing, and I ask you to stand fast!'

The four hundred or so young soldiers who had lined up on the deck of the *Birkenhead* obeyed him. A handful broke for safety, but that only served to emphasise the stolidity of the serried ranks who chose to stay, standing side by side as the ship sank towards the water. We do not know when and how the onrushing ocean finally overwhelmed the *Birkenhead*, but as the *Boy's Own Paper* told it, the young soldiers 'went down with her to their watery graves as if merely on parade'.

Every Victorian school child knew the story. Later immortalised in a poem by Rudyard Kipling, 'The Birkenhead Drill' was held to be the archetype for the 'stiff upper lip', that ideal of calm and stoic conduct in the face of hopeless circumstances which was the hallmark of the English gentleman. In fact, Colonel Seton who gave the order to 'stand fast' was Scottish, and the bulk of his men were Irish and Scots, many from the famous Highland regiment, the Black Watch.

When the liner *Titanic* sank in 1912, contempt would be poured on the men who saved their skins by getting into the lifeboats: they broke the rule established by the *Birkenhead* – 'Women and Children First'. And two years later, with the outbreak of the First World War, it was unquestioning, *Birkenhead*-style obedience that sent young men on both sides over the tops of the trenches to their deaths. The Emperor William I, who in 1871 unified Germany, decreed that the story of the *Birkenhead* should be 'read on parade at the head of every regiment in the Prussian service' – high praise, indeed, since the Prussians were renowned as the best-disciplined army in the world.

There was just one disturbing footnote to the apparently simple tale of heroism. Among the two hundred or so survivors fortunate enough to have drifted to shore in the warm ocean – avoiding horrifying shark attacks, which claimed numerous lives – was a young officer, Ensign Lucas, who recalled his final conversation with Colonel Seton.

'Perhaps we'll meet ashore, sir,' said Lucas.

'I do not think we shall, Lucas,' replied the colonel, 'as I cannot swim a stroke.'

So the *Birkenhead* drill was inspired by a non-swimming landlubber who had little option but to stand fast nobly on the deck – and who then imposed that option on his four hundred noble men.

INTO THE VALLEY OF DEATH

1854

O N   A   S U N N Y   M O R N I N G   L A T E   I N   O C T O B E R
1854, William Howard Russell, war correspondent of
The Times, found himself sitting among the stones and thistles of a Russian hillside with a ringside view of an ongoing
battle. 'The silence is oppressive,' he wrote. 'Between the
cannon bursts, one can hear the champing of bits and the
clink of sabres in the valley below.'

To his right, Russell could see water sparkling in the
harbour of Balaclava, 'a patch of blue sea' in a green landscape, and through this deceptively beautiful scenery rode the
Light Cavalry Brigade of the British army, their swords
unsheathed.

Looking through his field glasses, the reporter counted the British sabres – 607, he reckoned. 'They swept proudly past, glittering in the morning sun in all the pride and splendour of war.' But Russell could also see the menacing guns of the enemy, the Russians, stretched out along both sides and, most formidably, across the end of the valley. 'We could scarcely believe the evidence of our senses!' he wrote. 'Surely that handful of men were not going to charge an army in position?'

There had been a dreadful misunderstanding. High on the hillside, not far from where Russell was sitting, the British commander Lord Raglan had seen the Russian cavalry making off with some captured British guns. Now they were proceeding over the hills to one side of the valley, and Raglan instructed his own cavalry 'to advance rapidly to the front, and try to prevent the enemy carrying away the guns'.

But down on the floor of the valley, Lord Lucan, commander of the British cavalry, had no sight of the guns to which Raglan was referring. The only guns he could see were the ones straight ahead, and it was towards those that he now directed the Light Brigade. 'They advanced in two lines, quickening their pace as they closed towards the enemy,' wrote the horrified reporter. 'A more fearful spectacle was never witnessed than by those who, without the power to aid, beheld their heroic countrymen rushing to the arms of death.'

Russell was not then aware of the ambiguity of Raglan's order, which might have been checked or better explained if the British chain of command had been communicating more clearly with each other. The upper crust of aristocratic officers – many of whom had purchased their promotions to the elevated ranks they held – had been feuding ever since their arrival in the Crimea,* and Lucan was a particularly stubborn and peppery character. The man from *The Times* described the consequences in dreadful detail.

At the distance of 1200 yards the whole line of the enemy belched forth, from thirty iron mouths, a flood of smoke and flame, through which hissed the deadly balls. Their flight was marked by instant gaps in our ranks, by dead men and horses, by steeds flying wounded or riderless across the plain . . . Through the clouds of smoke we could see their sabres flashing as they rode up to the guns and dashed between them, cutting down the gunners as they stood.

The Light Brigade's heroism was in vain: 'Wounded men and dismounted troopers flying towards us told the sad tale . . . At twenty-five to twelve not a British soldier, except the dead and dying, was left in front of these bloody Muscovite guns.'

By Russell's count, less than two hundred of the six hundred brave cavalrymen who headed off down the mile-long valley made it back – and he filed his report on 'the melancholy loss' in a long handwritten dispatch that was carried back to England by ship and horse-borne courier, to be published in *The Times* of 14 November 1854. Never before

---

*In 1853 British and French forces invaded the Crimean Peninsula in southern Russia, ostensibly to protect the interests of Ottoman Turkey, but primarily to check Russian ambitions in the Black Sea and the Mediterranean.

had such graphic eyewitness details of war been conveyed so rapidly to the nation at home – and they caught the attention of the poet Alfred Tennyson, who, as he read the *Times* coverage, was particularly struck by the phrase 'hideous blunder'.

Tennyson had been working for months on a complicated love epic, *Maud: A Monodrama*, later famous for the refrain 'Come into the garden, Maud'. But on 2 December he took a few minutes' break to dash off what would become his most famous poem of all:

> *Half a league, half a league,**
> *Half a league onward,*
> *All in the valley of Death*
> *Rode the six hundred.*
> *'Forward, the Light Brigade!*
> *Charge for the guns!' he said:*
> *Into the valley of Death*
> *Rode the six hundred.*
>
> *'Forward, the Light Brigade!'*
> *Was there a man dismay'd ?*
> *Not tho' the soldier knew*
> *Some one had blunder'd:*
> *Their's not to make reply,*
> *Their's not to reason why,*
> *Their's but to do and die:*
> *Into the valley of Death*
> *Rode the six hundred.*

*A league is three miles – about five kilometres.

Cannon to right of them,
Cannon to left of them,
Cannon in front of them
Volley'd and thunder'd . . .
Into the jaws of Death,
Into the mouth of Hell
Rode the six hundred.

'The Charge of the Light Brigade' was published in the London *Examiner* on 9 December, less than seven weeks after the event it commemorated. Two years earlier the Victorians, as they were now calling themselves, had unquestioningly celebrated the discipline of the four hundred young recruits who stood to attention as the foundering *Birkenhead* took them to their deaths. Now Tennyson's poem captured the more complicated mixture of emotions inspired by the Light Brigade's blind obedience to orders – and this new perspective derived from the first-hand account of William Howard Russell watching from his Russian hillside among the stones and thistles.

In fact, *The Times's* casualty figures were incorrect. While only 195 men got back on horseback, many staggered back to camp later on foot. Modern research has suggested that just 110 of the six hundred died in action – Tennyson's poem, in other words, perpetuated a media mistake.

But Russell was the father of a new tradition. 'In his hands,' wrote his colleague Edwin Godkin of the *Daily News*, 'correspondence from the field really became a power before which generals began to quail . . . I cannot help thinking that the appearance of the special correspondent in the

Crimea . . . led to a real awakening of the official mind. It brought home to the War Office the fact that the public had something to say about the conduct of wars and that they are not the concern exclusively of sovereigns and statesmen.'

THE LADY OF THE LAMP AND
THE LADY WITH THE TEACUP
(PLUS THE ODD SIP OF BRANDY)

1854-5

FLORENCE NIGHTINGALE HEARD GOD'S VOICE
for the first time when she was sixteen years old. 'On 7
February, 1837,' she wrote, 'God spoke to me and called me to
His service.' Like Joan of Arc, Florence heard the words quite
clearly – but it took her seven years to work out what precise
form God's service should take: that she should go into hospitals to tend the sick.

The wealthy and elegantly fashionable Nightingale family
were horrified. To be a nurse was no occupation for a lady in
the early years of the nineteenth century. Hospitals were

degraded and dangerously infectious places – they gave off an odour of vomit and excrement that you could smell from the street. As for the women who were willing to work in such squalor, it was generally assumed that nurses were coarse and promiscuous, with a propensity to drink.

But God kept telling Florence what He wanted – she recorded the instructions in her painfully honest private notes and diaries – and at the age of thirty-three she took a job as superintendent of the Institute for the Care of Sick Gentlewomen in Distressed Circumstances in London's Harley Street. Caring for ageing governesses was a respectable job to which her family could not reasonably object (although, in fact, they did).

Then in October 1854 the war correspondents started writing home from the Crimea. 'It is with feelings of surprise and anger,' wrote Thomas Chinery, the Constantinople correspondent of *The Times*, 'that the public will learn that no sufficient medical preparations have been made for the proper care of the wounded. Not only are there not sufficient surgeons . . . there are no dressers or nurses to carry out the surgeon's directions.'

The very day *The Times* dispatch appeared, Florence contacted Sidney Herbert, the Secretary at War, offering to take a group of English nurses to Turkey – while Herbert himself, the husband of one of her dearest friends, was writing Florence a letter that crossed in the post: 'There is but one person in England that I know,' he wrote, 'who would be capable of organising and superintending such a scheme.'

This happy confidence was not shared by the resentful male staff in the military hospitals of Scutari in Turkey, where Florence and her thirty-eight nurses landed in

November 1854, just weeks after the Battle of Balaclava and the Charge of the Light Brigade. 'Abandon hope all ye who enter here' was the motto that Florence suggested for the rambling and dilapidated Barrack Hospital with its four grim miles of smelly wards. Her first order was for the supply of two hundred hard scrubbing brushes.

In the months that followed she rented a house near the hospital, installed large boilers and turned it into a laundry. Discovering that the food served to the wounded consisted mainly of gristly, over-boiled lumps of fatty meat, she arranged for Alexis Soyer, the celebrity chef of the day, to come out from London to reorganise the kitchens. Above all, she insisted on discipline, clean uniforms, and orderly working among her staff, laying the foundation for what would come to be known as the British nursing *profession*. In all of this, Florence set a personal example:

> *She is a 'ministering angel' without any exaggeration...* [declared John MacDonald, almoner of *The Times* Crimea Fund] *and as her slender form glides quietly along each corridor, every poor fellow's face softens with gratitude at the sight of her. When all the medical officers have retired for the night, and silence and darkness have settled down upon those miles of prostrate sick, she may be observed alone, with a little lamp in her hand, making her solitary rounds.*

A legend was born. Adored by the common soldiers and fêted by the newspapers, the lady with the lamp became a national heroine – and she hated it. 'The buz-fuz about my name,' she wrote, 'has done infinite harm.'

All glory, in Florence's view, must go to God. She refused a welcome-home reception because she felt deeply guilty that she had not achieved *more* for her patients, and she spent the rest of her life campaigning for army and hospital reform. She also fought to improve the training of midwives and the conditions inside maternity ('lying-in') hospitals, had a nursing school named after her, became an expert on sanitation and related health issues in India, and conducted a survey aiming to improve the lot of the 'Sick Poor' in workhouses.

Scarcely a day went by when Florence did not fire off a detailed letter to promote or protect one of her causes, and, throughout it all, she kept up her conversations with God, whom she eagerly looked forward to meeting face to face. When a friend dared suggest towards the end that death must come as something of a rest after a busy life, Miss Nightingale sat bolt upright on her pillows. 'Oh *no*,' she said with conviction, 'I am sure it is an *immense* activity.'

'I trust,' wrote William Howard Russell at the end of the Crimean War, 'that England will not forget one who nursed her sick, who sought out her wounded to aid and succour them, and who performed the last offices for some of her illustrious dead.'

The renowned war correspondent wrote many words in praise of Florence Nightingale, but on this occasion he was not referring to the Lady with the Lamp. Equally brave and caring was a Jamaican-born nurse of mixed race who had made her own way out to the Crimean War – Mary Seacole.

Mary would speak proudly of her ethnic mix – she often called herself 'the yellow woman'. Her mother was a

Jamaican 'doctress' who administered local folk remedies, her father a Scottish soldier in the local garrison: when she married, Mary went for an Englishman, the sickly Edwin Horatio Hamilton Seacole, godson of the famous Horatio Nelson.

On Mr Seacole's death in 1844, Mary had to fend for herself. Using the Creole healing skills she had learned from her mother, she turned her house in Kingston, Jamaica, into a convalescent home for invalid officers, picking up hints about Western medicine from visiting surgeons. On a visit to Panama in 1850 she won her own laurels as a 'doctress' when a cholera epidemic broke out, and she took charge of the local village, deploying the bag of medical supplies that she carried with her everywhere.

As a young woman, Mary had travelled several times to England – she financed one trip by the sale of her West Indian preserves and pickles – and in 1854, just approaching her fiftieth birthday, she found herself in London again. Reading the horrifying reports of conditions in the Crimea, she was moved, like Florence Nightingale, to contact the Secretary at War Sidney Herbert – but she received a very different response. Presenting herself at the front door of the minister's home, she endured long hours of contemptuous glances from the white servants who came and went in the great hall, and was then told, without any interview, that her services were not required.

She encountered similar rejection from the managers of the Crimean Fund that had already backed Florence Nightingale's mission to Scutari – Mary stood outside in the winter darkness, the tears streaming down her cheeks.

'Did these ladies shrink from accepting my aid,' she later wrote, 'because my blood flowed beneath a somewhat duskier skin than theirs?'

Mary got to nurse the soldiers just the same, though. With the help of Mr Day, a shopkeeper friend of her late husband, she booked a passage to the Black Sea, where she set up a Crimean version of her Kingston care centre. So rose, in the spring of 1855, in the shantytown of camp followers that gathered round the siege of Sebastopol, a cluster of buildings which Mary christened the 'British Hotel'. There was a kitchen, a canteen, sleeping quarters, stables and pens for livestock. The compound extended over more than an acre, and above Mr Day's trading store fluttered a large Union Jack.

Standing on a little hill just a mile from British headquarters, the British Hotel became a home-away-from-home for officers and men, offering cups of tea and generous servings of alcohol, Welsh rarebit, Irish stew – and, on a few eagerly awaited days a week, Mrs Seacole's celebrated rice pudding. Mary made her sausages from the pigs she kept in the yard, and, as the fame of her cooking spread, officers from the allied French army started dropping in for meals.

But it was her medical skills that made 'Mother Seacole' famous. She sold medicine to those who could afford it – and gave it to those who couldn't. She visited the bedsides of the sick, and, going a step further than Florence Nightingale whose work was in the military hospitals behind the lines, she even went out on to the battlefield. As the dead were being picked over by corpse plunderers, the portly form of Mrs Seacole could be seen administering sips of brandy to the suffering. She tended enemy Russians as well as the British and the French: when Sebastopol finally fell in 1855, she was the first woman to enter, by special permission of the allied command, carrying her medicine bag.

Peace brought disaster for the firm of Seacole and Day. The partnership had recently expanded their compound and had bought in new stocks of food and livestock. But with their customers, the allied troops, returning home, they had to sell to the local Russians for a fraction of their outlay. When Mary got back to England in 1856, she found herself facing bankruptcy proceedings.

But the war reporters had made Mother Seacole famous – they dubbed her 'the Creole with the Teacup' – and her plight was taken up by *The Times*, which championed a fund to assist her. *Punch* magazine organised a four-day military gala in her honour that was attended by eighty thousand people, and when Mary published her memoirs, *The Wonderful Adventures of Mrs Seacole in Many Lands*, her chirpy, no-nonsense style helped make the book an instant success.

Florence Nightingale had mixed feelings. 'Anyone who employs Mrs Seacole will introduce much kindness,' she remarked ' – also much drunkenness and improper conduct.' Still fighting her battle to make nurses respectable, Florence did not approve of Mary's raucous parties at the British Hotel: 'I will not call it a "bad house" – but something not very unlike it . . . She was very kind to the men and, what is more, to the Officers, and did some good and made many drunk.'

If the severe and driven Florence was a role model for the Victorian age, the plump and easy-going Mary provides more of a heroine for ours. 'The yellow woman' died wealthy and well loved in London in 1881 at the age of seventy-six, having proved the value of what she once described as 'that one common language of the whole world – smiles.'

CHARLES DARWIN AND THE
SURVIVAL OF THE FITTEST

1858

IMAGINE THAT YOU HAVE BEEN DEVOTING your principal energies for nearly twenty years to a Very Big Idea – a concept so revolutionary that it will transform the way the human race looks at itself. And then one morning, you open a letter from someone you scarcely know (someone, to be honest, that you never took very seriously) to discover that he has come up with exactly the same idea – and that he has picked you as the person to help him announce it to the world.

This was the dilemma that confronted Charles Darwin in June 1858 as he opened a thin, well wrapped package from Ternate, an island in the Dutch East Indies. He could recognise the handwriting of Alfred Russel Wallace, a railway surveyor-turned-naturalist who made his living selling specimens to richer collectors – a year or so back Darwin had asked him to track down some Malayan poultry skins for him.

But on this occasion, Wallace was not peddling specimens. He was asking Darwin to read a short, handwritten essay about natural selection. During a bout of malaria that February, the naturalist had got to thinking about the life-and-death struggle between existence and extinction in beasts and plants; about the need to adapt; about the selective breeding of domestic and farmyard animals to improve or alter their characteristics, and about the way that species diverge into different forms – all the ingredients of what would come to be known as 'evolution'.

'I never saw a more striking coincidence!' exclaimed the mortified Darwin. 'If Wallace had my MS [manuscript] sketch written out in 1842 he could not have made a better short abstract [summary].'

In June 1842, Darwin, then thirty-three, had sketched out his own ideas about evolution. Dinosaur discoveries and other geological research had pushed him towards the concept of the earth undergoing long, slow changes over the millennia. A five-year journey in his twenties on the research vessel *Beagle* had shown him how different forms of life adapted to different environments, most notably in the Galapagos Islands. And then in 1838 he had first laid eyes on an ape, an orang-utan, at London Zoo, and had started to make notes on her human-like emotions.

But the young man could see the bitter controversy towards which his thinking was leading – the idea that mankind was not created by God in a single day as the Bible described, but was, rather, shaped gradually in a long chain of descent that linked human beings to other species, including apes. Darwin himself found the idea deeply shocking – 'It is like confessing to murder,' he told a friend – and he reflected on the persecution handed out to the early astronomers who had dared to suggest that the earth revolved around the sun.

Such fears had held Charles Darwin back for nearly twenty years. He kept delaying publication, looking for one more piece of evidence to protect himself and his theory from the widespread outrage he anticipated – and now Wallace's essay meant, as Darwin wrote to the great geologist Charles Lyell, that 'all my originality, whatever it may amount to, will be smashed'.

Wallace had asked Darwin to forward his essay to Lyell if he approved of it, and, despite his disappointment, Darwin did the honourable thing. He could have destroyed the letter and pretended it had never arrived. He could have delayed doing anything, while rushing ahead with his own publication. Instead he passed it on – 'I hope you will approve of Wallace's sketch,' he wrote, 'that I may tell him what you say.'

Honour was rewarded. Lyell conferred with the botanist Joseph Hooker who decided that the groundbreaking ideas of both Wallace *and* Darwin should be presented side by side as soon as possible – at the very next meeting of the Linnean Society.* Alphabetically and chronologically, Darwin took precedence in the memorable double presentation of

*Britain's pre-eminent biology fellowship, named after the Swedish naturalist Carl Linnaeus, the father of modern plant and animal classification.

1 July 1858 – one of the great moments in the history of science – and some have claimed that this was a fix. Lyell and Hooker were both old friends of Darwin, and had been pushing the reluctant author to publish for years.

But when, weeks later in the Far East, Wallace found out that Lyell and Hooker had, without consulting him, assigned him the role of junior co-discoverer, he was all generosity, graciously thanking Hooker for the presentation that was 'so favourable to myself'. If he felt any resentment, he never once betrayed it. At the age of thirty-five the former railway surveyor, who had started his studies in the free libraries of Welsh mechanics' institutes, continued his researches to embark on a public career that would make him one of the best-known naturalists of his time – 'the Grand Old Man of Science', as he was often described. He also campaigned for socialism, spiritualism, the reform of the House of Lords and the Church of England, votes for women, the proper design of museums, the redistribution of land through the breaking up of the great noble estates, early 'green belts' (as we would call them) and the protection of historic monuments. Seldom short of a provocative and forward-looking idea, Wallace suggested that rather than going on strike, disgruntled employees should club together to buy out their bosses and prove they could do a better job themselves.

Darwin went on to become the grand old man of evolution, pushed by Wallace's challenge finally to write his masterpiece *The Origin of Species*,* which was published in

*Full title: *On the Origin of Species by Means of Natural Selection, or the Preservation of Favoured Races in the Struggle for Life.*

November 1859 and has never been out of print since. Sharing so many ideas, the two men who might have been fierce enemies actually became warm friends, treating each other with genuine respect. As the principal protagonists of what came to be known as the 'survival of the fittest' theory, with all its competitive, dog-eat-dog connotations, Darwin and Wallace illustrated how generosity can be the cleverest survival technique of all.

THE GREAT STINK – AND THE
TRAGEDY OF THE PRINCESS ALICE

1878

Dead hogges, dogges, cats and well-flayed carrion horses,
Their noisome corpses soyled the water's courses.
Both swines and stable dung, beast-guts and garbage,
Street-dust, with gardners' weeds and rotten herbage.
And from these waters' filthy putrefaction,
Our meat and drink were made, which breeds infection.
The River Thames described in 1632
by John Taylor, 'the Water Poet'

DUMPING YOUR RUBBISH IN THE RIVER
Thames was a long-cherished London tradition. In 1357

King Edward III complained of the 'fumes and other abominable stenches' this caused – he banned butchers from fouling the water with entrails from the beasts they slaughtered. Henry VIII attempted a total ban on dumping of any sort. But the Thames grew more polluted with every generation, and with the coming of the Industrial Revolution it became positively poisonous. Cement works and factories poured their effluent into the river, and the development of improved water closets made things worse. By the middle of the nineteenth century some 250 tons of human excrement were being flushed, daily, into the tidal flow.

Matters came to a head in the hot dry summer of 1858 when Parliament draped its windows with sheets soaked in chloride of lime in a vain attempt to combat what newspapers described as the 'Great Stink'. Legislators had to abandon the building as unusable. Fleeing from the Chamber, his nose buried in a scented handkerchief, the fastidious Benjamin Disraeli resolved on action. As Chancellor of the Exchequer he made funds available for an ambitious scheme to 'embank' the river.

The Thames's embankments, constructed in the 1860s, were the brainchild of Joseph Bazalgette, a friend of Brunel who, like Brunel, was the English-born son of a French immigrant family – in Bazalgette's case, of Huguenot descent. He reorganised London's thirteen hundred miles of sewers so they drained into a superhighway of gigantic pipes that ran alongside the water. On top of these were built the wide roads and tree-lined promenades of the Victoria, Albert and Chelsea Embankments – while, below the surface, the city's rechannelled sewage was carried

eastwards to the mouth of the river, where the tide was supposed to sweep it away.

The trouble was that the massive new culverts did not
extend that far downstream. Twice every twenty-four hours,
at high tide, two massive apertures at Barking and Crossness
spewed out 75 million gallons of untreated sewage on either
side of the river – with tragic consequences in 1878, when the
pleasure boat *Princess Alice* collided with the *Bywell Castle*, a
merchant steamer, not far from Woolwich.

The collision in itself was tragic enough – over 650
drowned. It was the worst single disaster in Thames history.
But one hour before the collision the outfalls at Barking and
Crossness had released their 75 million gallons into the tide,
and, as one correspondent to *The Times* described it, there
was 'projected into the river two continuous columns of
decomposed fermenting sewage, hissing like soda water with
baneful gases'.

'The water was very dreadful and nasty,' reported one witness at the subsequent coroner's inquest. 'Both for taste and
smell it was something [he] could hardly describe,' said
another. One survivor reckoned he owed his life to immediately vomiting up everything he had swallowed, but others
were not so fortunate. After the ghastly experience of struggling for life in the noxious brown soup, the papers reported
mysterious instances of paralysis, illness and a rate of fatality
which, as *The Times* put it, was 'exceedingly large' if judged 'as
the mere effect of an immersion in water on a fine summer
evening'.

Then watermen noticed that the bodies of the dead were
rising to the surface after only six days. The expected period

for a corpse to float was nine ‒ and these bodies were more bloated than usual. They could not fit into conventional coffins. Covered in a strange slime, which reappeared when washed off, their stench was so revolting that the dockers hired to move them went on strike for better money. The virulently chemical nature of the river was suggested by the way that the dead women's dresses changed from blue to violet. One pharmaceutical chemist offered his own analysis: while diluted sewage, 'say one drop in 10,000', was known to produce fevers like typhoid, concentrated and actively decomposing sewage produced sulphuretted hydrogen that was 'relatively as fatal as prussic acid'.

This was the other side ‒ the price, indeed ‒ of all the mass-produced wonders in Prince Albert's Crystal Palace. The Victorian spirit of free enterprise and devil-take-the-hindmost was summed up in Samuel Smiles's *Self-Help* (published in 1859, the year after the Great Stink).* Typhoid fever was killing nearly fifteen hundred Londoners a year; in the course of one thirty-five-year cycle, outbreaks of cholera, another disease of polluted water, claimed thirty-six thousand more. But the idea that government should intervene was still seen by many as an unacceptable infringement of freedom. 'We prefer to take our chance of cholera and the rest,' declared *The Times*, '[rather] than be bullied into health.'

The sinking of the *Princess Alice* (named after Queen Victoria's third daughter) did produce some reform. The rules of navigation on the river were more rigidly enforced,

---

*Self-Help was published on the same day, and by the same publisher (John Murray), as Charles Darwin's *Origin of Species*.

and the Metropolitan Board of Works went back to Joseph (now Sir Joseph) Bazalgette for a new sewage strategy – to extract the solid waste and transport it far out to sea in a fleet of sludge boats. So the old Thames tradition of dumping survived more grandly than ever.

LORD ROSEBERY'S HISTORICAL
HOWLER

1887

I N 1 8 8 7 QUEEN VICTORIA HAD BEEN FIFTY
years on the throne, and Lord Rosebery wanted to give her
a present to mark the occasion. The British public were celebrating with a jubilee (the word came from 'jobel', the Old
Testament celebration that took its name from the blowing
of the ram's horn trumpet), but Lord Rosebery wanted to
offer a personal tribute. He had served as Victoria's Foreign
Secretary the previous year and was widely tipped as a future
Prime Minister.* What better gift than some memento of

*Archibald Philip Primrose, 5th Earl of Rosebery, became Prime
Minister in 1894, but did not live up to his promise, resigning the

England's only other great and long-reigning queen, Elizabeth I? So Rosebery dispatched a dainty miniature portrait of 'Gloriana', with a letter expressing the hope that Her Majesty would accept this remembrance of her illustrious predecessor.

Queen Victoria was most touched. The 68-year-old monarch had a soft spot for the dashing young grandee – forty years old and noted for his eloquence. She wrote to Rosebery next day, thanking him for his 'kind and most valuable present, accompanied by such flattering words . . . I am delighted to possess this exquisite gem which I *intend* to *wear*' – underlining the two words to emphasise her pleasure.

But there was one problem. As a stickler for sometimes inconvenient truth, Queen Victoria felt she had to remind Lord Rosebery: 'I have no sympathy with my great Predecessor, descended as I am from her rival Queen, whom she so cruelly sacrificed.'

Lord Rosebery had made the common historical error of forgetting that the modern British monarchy does not descend from Queen Elizabeth I, who had no descendants, but from Mary Queen of Scots, who was executed by Elizabeth (see *Great Tales*, vol. 2, p. 150). It was Mary's son James who brought the Stuart dynasty south after Elizabeth died in 1603.

---

following year. He is better remembered for his empire-based foreign policy in the tradition of 'splendid isolation' – he invented the phrase 'the British Commonwealth of Nations' – and as an owner of racehorses. He won the Derby three times. He was one of the last British prime ministers to sit in the House of Lords.

ANNIE BESANT AND 'PHOSSY JAW' – THE STRIKE OF THE MATCH GIRLS

1888

I will speak for the dumb. I will speak of the small to the great, and of the feeble to the strong. I will speak for all the despairing silent ones.

Motto of Annie Besant's halfpenny weekly, The Link

'PHOSSY JAW' WAS A DEADLY OCCUPATIONAL hazard that afflicted young women who worked in Victorian match factories, where the ends of the matchsticks were dipped into a combustible white phosphorus paste.

The disease started with a toothache, followed by painful and unpleasant-smelling abscesses as the bone tissue rotted away. In its final stages, the remains of the phosphorus-infected jaw glowed in the dark a greenish-yellowy white. Surgical removal might save the sufferer's life; otherwise, convulsions, 'inflammation of the brain' and death through organ failure would inevitably result.

In June 1888 the journalist Annie Besant exposed the terrible life of the match girls in her campaigning weekly, *The Link*. At the Bryant & May factory in east London, she reported, teenagers were paid only a few shillings a week, from which fines could be deducted by the management for such offences as talking too much, dropping matches, or going to the toilet without permission. The girls worked from 6.30 a.m. in summer (8 in winter) to 6 p.m., and were fined half a day's pay if they were late. Bryant & May, meanwhile, were paying huge dividends to their shareholders, so that a £5 share was valued at over £18.

A few days after her article appeared (under the title 'White Slavery in London'), Annie Besant heard female voices calling her name outside the office of *The Link* in Fleet Street. The match girls had come to see her. The Bryant & May management had asked them to sign letters saying they were happy and contented – the firm was planning to sue Annie for libel – and the women had refused.

'You had spoke up for us,' explained one, 'and we weren't going back on you.'

Soon afterwards one of their leaders was sacked, and all fourteen hundred match girls came out on strike. They had no union organisation, and they turned to Annie for help.

'A pretty hubbub we created,' Annie later recalled. 'We asked for money, and it came pouring in; we registered the girls for strike pay, wrote articles, roused the clubs, held public meetings . . . '

Annie Besant pioneered techniques of protest that are in use to this day. She took a delegation of the girls to lobby the House of Commons in their ragged, East End clothes, so the press could not help but note 'the contrast between these poor "white slaves" and their opulent sisters' of the West End. As the girls spoke to MPs 'in their own words', one pretty thirteen-year-old whipped off her bonnet to reveal a bald scalp from carrying heavy wooden palettes on her head.

Bryant & May were forced to climb down. They agreed to a package that included the abolition of all deductions and fines, and the provision of a breakfast room for their workers. The girls returned to work next day, victorious – and, following a further campaign in which Annie also took part, white phosphorus was eventually banned. It was replaced by red, which worked just as well in matches and had no deleterious side effects.

The strike of the match girls was a landmark in British labour history – it helped inspire the formation of trades unions all over the country, and it provided an early grass-roots triumph in the struggle for women's rights. But for Annie Besant, forty years old in 1888, it was just one in a lifetime of battles. In her twenties she had walked away from Frank Besant, a stiff-necked Lincolnshire vicar who made it a condition of their marriage that she attend holy communion every Sunday. In her thirties she was convicted, and narrowly escaped prison, for publishing a treatise on birth control that was deemed obscene. Following her victory with the match girls, she turned to the mystic cult of theosophy and became interested in the Eastern religions.

This took her out to India, where she campaigned for Indian Home Rule and adopted Indian dress, a white sari and white sandals – white being the Hindu colour of mourning. She was in mourning, she explained, for all the harm that British rule had done to the country, and the British returned the compliment by interning her for a while. Annie Besant died in Madras at the age of eighty-six, fighting so long as she had strength for all the despairing silent ones.

DIAMOND JUBILEE – THE
EMPIRE MARCHES BY

1897

A S QUEEN VICTORIA RODE OUT OF BUCKINGHAM
Palace on a sunny June morning in 1897, she leant from
her carriage to press a specially mounted button, which,
through the ingenuity of the electric telegraph, dispatched a
greeting on her behalf to every corner of her worldwide
Empire. Within sixteen minutes the first answer – from
Ottawa in Canada – came clicking back.

The electric telegraph was just one of the many miracles
that had transformed life in the sixty eventful years since the
young Queen had received the Archbishop of Canterbury in
her dressing-gown. 'Slavery has been abolished,' wrote her
reforming Prime Minister, William Ewart Gladstone,

proudly. 'A criminal code that disgraced the statute book has been effectually reformed.' Most men (but no women) could now vote by secret ballot. Free education was available to almost everyone. Gaslight illuminated homes and streets. One penny would buy a postage stamp which, when licked and applied to an envelope, would carry your letter to almost any corner of the country overnight. People were generally richer than their parents – and most would live longer, thanks to medical advances like anaesthesia and antiseptics. They could also travel quicker and further, thanks to railways and steamships – and a lucky few now considered it their right to take at least one holiday a year.

Queen Victoria had played no personal role in any of these transformations, over which she had presided as a sometimes grudging head of state. Overcome with grief at the premature death of her beloved Albert in 1861, she had withdrawn from the world for many years and was only reluctantly coaxed back to perform a few of her public duties – and then in a style that was dripping with disapproval. Of the many photographs of Britain's longest reigning monarch, only one shows her smiling.

But the grumpier the old Queen became, the more the world loved her. By 1897, aged seventy-eight, Victoria was by far the most famous woman on earth, her name bestowed on cities, rivers, lakes, bays and great waterfalls all over the planet. Ten years previously her half-century had been marked with a Golden Jubilee. Now the government proclaimed that her sixty years on the throne be celebrated as her Diamond Jubilee, and the Empire assembled in London to do her homage: the streets were fragrant with fresh-sawn green pine, as miles of wooden stands were thrown up to accommodate the spectators.

Headed by the tallest officer in the British army, six feet eight inches in his bare feet and riding a gigantic charger, the procession of sailors, military bands, clattering horses and colourfully garbed fighting men was forty-five minutes long. The Empire – almost literally – passed by. From Canada they came, from Australia, Africa, India, Borneo, Fiji, Hong Kong – Britain ruled nearly a quarter of the earth's land-mass in 1897, eleven million square miles (28,000,000 square kilometres) coloured red in the atlases of the day. Bringing up the rear, hunched in her carriage, came the little widow in black to whom a quarter of the world's inhabitants paid homage.

The bells of St Paul's fell silent as the procession stopped in front of the cathedral for an open-air service – the Queen Empress was too lame to get down from her carriage. Lined up on the steps the assembled clerics and choirboys sang their way lustily through the hymns, in the last of which the Queen's carriage was supposed to start moving off. But, recalled the Bishop of London:

> the other carriages waited, and when the hymn was over there was a pause of intolerable silence. The Archbishop of Canterbury, with splendid audacity and disregard of decorum, interpreted what was in everyone's mind, and cried out 'Three cheers for the Queen!'
>
> Never were cheers given with such startling unanimity and precision. All the horses threw up their heads at the same moment, and gave a little quiver of surprise. When the cheers were over, the

band and chorus, by an irresistible impulse, burst into 'God Save the Queen'.

Scarcely was the Queen round the corner when 'one of the choir boys, unable to restrain himself any longer, dashed from his place, leapt down the steps and filled his pockets with the gravel on which the wheels of the carriage had rested'.

As the boy sought to grasp the fleeting magic of the moment, operators of the recently invented movie camera were doing precisely the same. The 'cinematograph' had come to London only the previous year, but in June 1897 more than twenty rival newsreel companies set up their cameras along the ceremonial route. Pondering how to capture the splendours of the long, moving procession on film, they came up with a swivel device that would enable the previously immovable camera to swing from side to side and capture the full panorama. So the cinema's staple 'panning' shot owes its origin to Queen Victoria.

SLAUGHTER ON SPION KOP

1900

The tumult and the shouting dies;
The Captains and the Kings depart . . .
Far-called, our navies melt away;
On dune and headland sinks the fire:
Lo, all our pomp of yesterday
Is one with Nineveh and Tyre!

. . .

Lord God of Hosts, be with us yet,
Lest we forget – lest we forget!

THE POET RUDYARD KIPLING FELT UNEASY AT the boastful pomp and circumstance of the Diamond Jubilee celebrations. Until 1897 the author of the *Jungle Books* (and later of the *Just So Stories*) had been known as a jingoistic* cheerleader of imperialism. But now he composed a doom-laden ode that he entitled 'Recessional',† comparing Britain's worldwide dominions to the once proud Old Testament empires of Assyria that crumbled into sand.

Kipling ended each verse with the warning 'Lest we forget!' and in less than three years the warning proved justified. In 1899 Britain was pouring troops into southern Africa in an attempt to discipline the Boers, the Dutch-speaking farmers who had settled the Cape before the arrival of the English, and they encountered bitter resistance. The Boers correctly interpreted British interference as a land-grab – vast deposits of gold and diamonds had recently been discovered beneath the Boer territory of the Transvaal – and when the fighting started, their local knowledge gave them the upper hand.

One night in January 1900 some two thousand British troops, many of them conscripts from Liverpool serving in Lancashire regiments, were sent scampering up a *kopje* (little hill) known as the *spion* (lookout), about a dozen miles from the town of Ladysmith in Natal. The plan was to secure,

---

*The word comes from the Victorian music-hall song – 'We don't want to fight, but by jingo if we do, we've got the ships, we've got the men, and got the money too.'
†A hymn sung at the end of a church service, as the choir and clergy leave the church.

under cover of darkness, a position from which they could fire down on the Boers. But next morning it became tragically clear that the opposite was the case. When the sun burned off the mist around 8 a.m., the British found themselves exposed to the enemy's pitiless fire streaking down from the surrounding hilltops that were higher than Spion Kop. 'The Boers was up above us, see,' one survivor told the author Thomas Pakenham many years later. 'They'd got us in a trap.'

In the interests of camouflage, the British army had recently switched its combat uniform from red to khaki, but the men on top of Spion Kop were sitting targets. With just twenty shovels between them, they had only been able to dig themselves a shallow trench across the top of the rocky hill, and the Boers were deadly shots.

'Shells rained in among us,' recalled another old survivor. 'The most hideous sights were exhibited – men blown to atoms, joints torn asunder. Headless bodies, trunks of bodies. Awful. Awful. You dared not lift your head above the rock or you were shot dead at once.'

Watching the slaughter was a young war correspondent for the *Morning Post* who bravely made his way to the foot of the hill. 'Men were staggering along alone, or supported by comrades, or crawling on hands and knees,' wrote the 26-year-old Winston Churchill. 'The splinters and fragments of shell had torn and mutilated in the most ghastly manner.'

Helping the wounded was another gigantic figure of twentieth-century history, Mohandas Gandhi, the inspiration of the Indian independence movement who was later known as the Mahatma ('Great Soul'). Then a 28-year-old barrister working in Durban's Indian community, Gandhi had volunteered his services as a stretcher-bearer, and would win a British campaign medal for his work in raising an ambulance corps of more than a thousand Indians.

By the time nightfall brought merciful relief from the bombardment, the young British commander Alec Thorneycroft had had enough. 'Poor boys, poor boys,' he kept muttering, giving the order to evacuate. 'Better six battalions safely off the hill than a mop up in the morning.'

A shortage of signal-lamp oil meant Thorneycroft had not received a crucial message – the news that guns and reinforcements were on their way. Had the British held their ground they could have retained Spion Kop, since the Boers had suffered casualties themselves and were almost out of ammunition. They could not have sustained another day's attack and many of the farmers were preparing to ride away. Three hundred and twenty-two British soldiers had died, with 563 wounded, for nothing.

Six years later the fruitless sacrifice received its most famous memorial. Founded in 1892, Liverpool Football Club won its second League Championship in 1906 and decided to celebrate by building extra room for spectators at its Anfield ground – a tall embankment that could pack more than twenty thousand standing behind one of the goals. Ernest Edwards, the editor of the *Liverpool Post and Echo*, had a suggestion to make: that Anfield's new embankment should be named 'Spion Kop' as a memorial to 'all those local lads of ours' who gave their lives in Natal.

And so the 'Kop' became the inspirational heart of one of the most successful teams in English soccer history. Twenty minutes after kick-off on 1 September 1906, Joe Hewitt gave Liverpool the lead against Stoke City when he scored the first ever goal in front of the Kop, and Liverpool has gone on to win sixteen more League titles and five European Cups – 'Walk on, walk on, with hope in your heart, and you'll never walk alone . . .'

Well, not quite alone, for Edwards's idea had a London inspiration. In 1904 the Woolwich Arsenal football team, largely composed of military men and munitions workers at the Royal Arsenal workshops in Woolwich, southeast London, had decided to name their high new cinder embankment 'Spion Kop'. The name did not survive Arsenal's 1913 move across the river to their new stadium at Highbury, but by then the grieving munitions workers had inspired no less than sixteen other clubs, as well as Liverpool, to name their home hills after the men who scaled Spion Kop and did not come down again.*

*The kops of English football: Anfield (Liverpool); Bloomfield Road (Blackpool); Bramall Lane (Sheffield United); County Ground (Northampton Town); Elland Road (Leeds United); Highfield Road (Coventry City); Hillsborough (Sheffield Wednesday); Home Park (Plymouth Argyle); Leeds Road (Huddersfield Town); Meadow Lane (Notts County); Prenton Park (Tranmere Rovers); Racecourse Ground (Wrexham); Recreation Ground (Chesterfield); St Andrews (Birmingham City); Valley Parade (Bradford City); Filbert Street (Leicester City); York Street (Boston United).

EDWARD VII AND THE
ENTENTE CORDIALE

1903

TWO HUNDRED THOUSAND BRITISH TROOPS
versus sixty thousand Boers – the war in South Africa
should have been a walkover. But the elusive guerrilla tactics
of the local Afrikaner farmers drove the British commander
Lord Kitchener to repressive measures – the Boer farms
were burned, their livestock was looted, and their dispossessed women and children were 'concentrated' into camps
along the railway lines.

Surrounded by barbed wire, with inadequate food and
germ-laden water, these 'concentration camps' became
Britain's shame – some 24,000 Boer women and children
and 14,000 interned Africans died in epidemics of dysentery,

measles and enteric fever. Britain eventually 'won' the South African War (fought from 1899 to 1902), forcing the Boers into what became the Union of South Africa. But it was a poor way to start the new century. 'When children are treated in this way and dying,' commented David Lloyd George, the campaigning Liberal MP, 'we are simply ranging the deepest passions of the human heart against British rule in Africa.'

The Boers were no saints. Among the 'freedoms' for which they were fighting was the right to treat the native, non-white inhabitants of southern Africa as slaves – their twentieth-century Afrikaner descendants would devise the segregationist system of apartheid. But their fight against the might of the British Empire made them heroes in Europe. When Britain's new King, Edward VII, visited Paris in May 1903, hostile shouts of *'Vive les Boers!'* came ringing from the crowds.

'The French don't like us,' commented one of his courtiers. 'Why should they?' the King replied.

Fifty-nine years old when his mother Queen Victoria died in January 1901, Edward VII was determined to make the most of the short time left to him as King. He possessed an old-fashioned confidence that his job involved having an impact on national policy – and the test of that came on this same visit to the unwelcoming city of Paris, where cries of *'Vive Jeanne d'Arc!'* mingled with those in support of the Boers.

Edward liked France. As Prince of Wales, he had made many visits to the capital, where he had tried to disguise his identity by travelling as the 'Duke of Lancaster'. But his portly, bearded form was unmistakable, and the French detectives assigned to shadow him spent many a long afternoon waiting outside the apartments of countesses and courtesans – all of them beautiful.

Now King Edward applied his seductive royal glamour to the affairs of nations. 'Ah, Mademoiselle,' he said loudly to the actress Jeanne Granier, kissing her hand when he met her on his first evening in Paris, 'I remember how I applauded you in London where you represented all the grace, all the esprit of France.' Next day's papers reported the King's delight at being once more 'in this beautiful city', and when he got to the Town Hall he said it all – and more besides – in the language of his audience: Paris, he declared, was a city *'où je me trouve toujours comme si j'étais chez moi.'*

Edward VII had a warm and genial voice, husky with the brandy and cigars of which he was so fond. When speaking in public, he had always conveyed the impression that he found life a matter of the utmost enjoyment, and when this was allied in May 1903 to his fluent and self-confident French, the effect was electric. His claim to be feeling 'at home' received 'a tremendous ovation', recorded his adviser Frederick Ponsonby. 'He now seemed to have captured Paris by storm. From that moment everything changed wherever he went. Not only the King but all of the suite were received with loud and repeated cheering.' Crowds blocked the path of the royal carriage shouting, '*Vive Édouard!*' '*Notre bon Édouard!*' and even '*Vive notre roi!*' As Paris's new hero embarked for the Channel, the newspapers used words like *passionnant* to describe the popular farewell.

From the days of William III and Marlborough to the

time of Napoleon (the 1690s until 1815), France and Britain had been locked in recurring conflict – a second Hundred Years War. But they had collaborated against Russia in the Crimea (1853–6) and they had recently found common cause in their fears about the rising power of Germany. Edward VII did not invent the rapprochement, but his spectacular success in Paris forced the pace. Serious negotiation started that summer, and on 8 April 1904 the Entente Cordiale was signed in London.

The 'warm understanding' resolved a set of relatively minor trade and territorial differences that had been aggravating relations between Britain and France – largely to do with who controlled what in various corners of their empires. It was not a military alliance. But it ended Britain's standoffish policy of 'splendid isolation' from her European neighbours, and now appears a prelude to the great events of the twentieth century. In two consuming and murderous world wars, British troops would find themselves fighting in Europe . . . in the defence of France.

CELLAR MURDERER CAUGHT BY
WIRELESS – DR CRIPPEN

1910

Dr HAWLEY HARVEY CRIPPEN THOUGHT HE had got away with it. Early in 1910 he killed his wife Cora, having first sedated her – and maybe half-poisoned her – with hyoscine hydrobromide. Using his medical knowledge, Crippen then dismembered her body, disposing of her head, skeleton and internal organs so they were never found. He buried what was left in the cellar of their home at 39 Hilldrop Crescent in Holloway, north London, and started a new life there with his lover, Ethel le Neve, who was sighted about this time wearing Cora's jewellery.

When the police came round, prompted by suspicious neighbours, Crippen said Cora had gone to America. Then he and Ethel fled to Belgium, where they boarded a liner, the SS *Montrose*, sailing from Antwerp to Canada. Crippen shaved off his moustache and posed as John Philo Robinson, travelling with his sixteen-year-old son (Ethel in disguise). Unfortunately for the couple, the *Montrose* was equipped with one of the first of the Marconi Telegraph Company's new 'wireless' machines.

'Have strong suspicion that Crippen London cellar murderer and accomplice are amongst saloon passengers,' telegraphed the *Montrose's* captain, Henry Kendall, on 22 July, as the liner sailed past the tip of Cornwall. 'Moustache shaved off, growing a beard. Accomplice dressed as a boy, voice, manner and build undoubtedly a girl.'

Captain Kendall had been reading the newspapers. A week earlier they had reported how Inspector Walter Drew of Scotland Yard had searched 39 Hilldrop Crescent following the flight of the couple, and had discovered a set of headless and bizarrely filleted human body parts – presumably the remains of Cora – buried beneath the coal-cellar floor. On receipt of Captain Kendall's cable, the detective headed for Liverpool to board SS *Laurentic*, a mail steamer due to reach Montreal three days ahead of the *Montrose*.

Captain Kendall's ship-to-shore broadcast was the first time that wireless telegraphy, developed by Guglielmo Marconi in the 1890s, had been used to catch a murderer. It also provoked the first tabloid melodrama of the twentieth century, since details of the captain's wireless message were leaked to the press. As reporters leapt on board the *Laurentic* with Inspector Drew, readers around the world were able to follow the race across the Atlantic day by day.

On the *Montrose*, meanwhile, Captain Kendall kept the story to himself. He made friends with the unsuspecting 'Robinsons', wiring details of their doings to the outside world. When he revealed that Dr Crippen was reading the thriller *The Four Just Men*, it sealed the fame of its author, Edgar Wallace.

The press was on hand when Inspector Drew, having arrived first in Montreal, disguised himself as a pilot and went on board the *Montrose*. 'Let me introduce you,' said the ever helpful Captain Kendall (who later published his memoirs, *Ship's Log*).

As 'Mr Robinson' extended his hand, Inspector Drew promptly grabbed it, whipping off his pilot's cap. 'Good morning, Dr Crippen,' said the detective (who would also publish his own memoir, *I Caught Crippen*). 'Do you remember me? I'm Inspector Drew from Scotland Yard.'

'Thank God it's over' was the fugitive's reported response. 'The suspense has been too great. I couldn't stand it any longer.'

In the trial that followed, the quiet-spoken doctor, with his wire-framed spectacles and droopy moustache, scarcely emerged as an ogre. He had sold homeopathic remedies, managed a deaf institute and tried his hand at dentistry in a succession of failed careers that his shrewish wife Cora used to deride. The hen-pecked Crippen consummated his relationship with Ethel only after he found Cora – a would-be opera singer – in bed with another man, and his main purpose at his trial was to avoid saying anything that might incriminate the woman he now loved.

In this he succeeded. Ethel le Neve was acquitted.

Crippen was found guilty on 22 October, and spent the weeks until his execution exchanging ardent love letters with Ethel. Coupled with his humdrum appearance, his devotion somehow made his crime of passion, dismembering his wife's remains in a net-curtained suburban street, all the more shocking. He was hanged at Pentonville Prison on 23 November 1910.

Ethel le Neve changed her name after her acquittal and managed to avoid attention for the rest of her life. But her lover Dr Crippen, the Cellar Murderer, remains to this day one of the star waxwork attractions in Madame Tussaud's Chamber of Horrors.

'I MAY BE SOME TIME . . .' – THE
SACRIFICE OF CAPTAIN OATES

1912

LAWRENCE OATES WAS A SCRUFFY-LOOKING character, often to be seen in a battered old Aquascutum raincoat that he buttoned tightly round his neck. He was wearing it when he arrived at the London berth of the *Terra Nova*, Captain Robert Scott's expedition ship that was about to weigh anchor for the Antarctic in the spring of 1910. The crew 'never thought for one moment', according to the Irish explorer Tom Crean, 'that he was an officer'. 'But oh! he was a gentleman,' remembered Crean, 'quite a gentleman and always a gentleman.'

Educated at Eton and a Master of Foxhounds, Oates certainly had the resources of a gentleman – he contributed

£1000 (the equivalent of £66,000 today) to the funds of the Antarctic expedition. He was indeed an officer, the only horse expert in a group of mainly naval adventurers – they nicknamed him 'The Soldier'.* Oates's job was to care for the ponies on which the British were relying to carry food and fuel to their supply dumps along the route to the South Pole.

But Scott had not thought to send Oates to Siberia to purchase the ponies, whose strength was crucial to the success of the expedition. When the animals arrived, Oates was horrified to find they were a 'wretched load of crocks'. He complained bitterly to Scott, cataloguing their faults in his diary – 'knock knees . . . aged . . . wind-sucker . . . lame' – along with equally bad news: a wire from the Norwegian explorer Roald Amundsen announcing that he was heading for the Pole: 'I only hope they don't get there first,' Oates recorded gloomily, 'it will make us look pretty foolish after all the fuss we have made.'

To pull their sleighs the Norwegians were relying on a large number of dogs (over two hundred), which they planned to slaughter systematically as they went along, feeding the meat to the survivors. Scott considered this inhumane. He was counting on just thirty-two dogs, Oates's ponies and three new-fangled motor sledges to get his men within striking distance, at which point they would drag their own sledges to the Pole and then back to 'One Ton' Depot, so called after the amount of stores it contained.

*The captain's other nickname was 'Titus' after the notorious Oates (no relation) who stirred up national hysteria in the reign of Charles II over the so-called 'Popish Plot' (see *Great Tales*, vol. 2, pp. 220–5).

But this provoked another disagreement, since Oates felt they should site One Ton Depot closer to the Pole. He proposed killing the weakest of his ponies as meat to provide energy for the dogs – and the men – to move the contents of the depot a crucial ten miles or so closer to their destination.

'I have had more than enough of this cruelty to animals,' replied Scott, 'and I'm not going to defy my feelings for the sake of a few days' march.'

'I'm afraid you'll regret it, sir,' retorted Oates.

'Myself, I dislike Scott intensely,' the indignant Oates confided in a letter home to his mother, 'and would chuck the whole thing if it was not that we are a British Expedition and must beat those Norwegians . . . The fact of the matter is he is not straight; it is himself first, the rest nowhere, and when he has got all he can out of you, it is shift for yourself.'

Oates accurately pinpointed the ruthless streak in the self-obsessed Scott, and when the British reached the Pole on 18 January 1912 to discover that the Norwegians had, in fact, beaten them by more than a month, Oates made clear in his diary which expedition had been more rationally led: 'That man [Amundsen] must have had his head screwed on right . . . They seem to have had a comfortable trip with their dog teams – very different from our wretched man-hauling.'

Stumbling through ice and crevasses by day, shivering in damp sleeping-bags by night, the demoralised British team hauled their sledges back towards One Ton Depot, a 120-mile journey which they might have hoped to cover inside three weeks. But they were harassed by bitterly freezing weather – and by frostbite. Edgar Evans, the only member of the final five-man team who was not of the officer class, suc-cumbed to delirium, finally collapsing and dying after four hard weeks in which his fatigue and confusion had held the whole party back. 'The absence of poor Evans,' noted Scott unsentimentally, 'is a help to the commissariat [food supply].'

Now it was Oates's turn to hold the party back. He was already walking with a limp, the legacy of a wound he had sustained in the Boer War, and the frostbite in his feet was turning gangrenous. It slowed his walking pace and, worse, his preparation time every day, as he struggled for two hours with the agonising pain of pulling his boots over his feet.

'Poor Titus is the greatest handicap,' Scott confided to his diary. 'He keeps us waiting in the morning until we have partly lost the warming effect of our good breakfast . . . It is too pathetic to watch him.' Unable to pull, Oates would col-lapse on a sledge whenever the party halted. 'If we were all fit, I should have hopes of getting through,' wrote Scott in his diary on 6 March, 'but the poor Soldier has become a terri-ble hindrance.'

It was now seventeen days since Evans had died, but Oates insisted on carrying on. On 11 March Scott handed out thirty opium tablets to each man, a suicide dose; but if this was a hint, Oates declined to take it. Malnutrition and the agony of his frostbitten hands and feet may have clouded his mind. He kept going through the motions, wrestling with his boots every morning, staggering out into the freez-ing white blindness.

He was a brave soul [wrote Scott on the 17th]. *This was the end. He slept through the night before last, hoping not to wake,*

but he woke in the morning – yesterday. It was blowing a bliz-
zard. He said, 'I am just going outside and I may be some time.'
He went out into the blizzard and we have not seen him since . . .
We knew that poor Oates was walking to his death, but though we
tried to dissuade him, we knew it was the act of a brave man and
an English gentleman.

So Captain Oates passed into history. Scott and his other companions died some two weeks later, just eleven miles short of One Ton Depot – which raises several questions. Might they have survived if Scott had heeded Oates's advice to locate the depot further south? And might they possibly have been able to cover that further eleven miles if Captain Oates had made his sacrifice earlier – at the beginning of March, say – instead of lingering, 'a terrible hindrance' to his companions, until the 16th?

The truth has vanished long ago in the glaring white mist. The last words that Oates himself wrote were in his diary on 24 February 1912 – so everything we think we know about the last three weeks of his life, together with his now famous manner of dying, comes from the pen of Captain Scott, the man whom Oates described as 'not straight'.

THE KING'S HORSE AND
EMILY DAVISON

1913

O N 14 JUNE 1913 LONDONERS FLOCKED BY
the thousand to Epsom Downs in Surrey for an afternoon of beer and betting. It was Derby Day, and in the
stands with his binoculars was the King himself, George V,
the bearded son of the bearded Edward VII, whom he had
succeeded in 1910. The King owned one of the less fancied
entries, a colt named Anmer,* and as the horses reached the

---

*The Derby takes its name from the sporting Earl of Derby who
founded the race in 1780. Anmer was a wood where George V particularly enjoyed shooting, near the village of Anmer on the royal estate of
Sandringham in Norfolk.

halfway stage, the sharp bend at Tattenham Corner, Anmer had already fallen back in the chasing pack.

Suddenly there was a commotion in the crowd. 'I noticed a figure bob under the rails,' recounted one eyewitness in *The Times* next day. 'The horses were thundering down the course at a great pace bunched up against the rail.'

The figure was a forty-year-old university graduate and teacher, Emily Davison, a 'suffragette' – so called because of her campaigning for female suffrage, votes for women.

'The king's horse Anmer came up,' recounted another spectator, 'and Miss Davison went towards it. She put up her hand, but whether it was to catch hold of the reins or to protect herself I do not know. It was all over in a few seconds. The horse knocked the woman over with very great force, and then stumbled and fell, pitching the jockey violently onto the ground. Both he and Miss Davison were bleeding profusely.'

Anmer rolled over, got to his feet, and galloped off down the course to complete the race without his rider. The jockey, Herbert Jones, lay 'doggo' on the ground till the last horse had passed, then sat up gingerly – he had a bruised face and fractured rib, with mild concussion. But Emily Davison did not move. She lay crumpled and unconscious, thrown to the ground with such force that her spine had been fractured at the base of her skull. She never regained consciousness, and died four days later.

Emily Davison was a passionate member of the Women's Social and Political Union, led by Emmeline Pankhurst and her eldest daughter Christabel. The Pankhursts had campaigned for many years through the Independent Labour

Party, the predecessor of the modern Labour Party, until the ILP, fearing that middle- and upper-class women would vote for their opponents, had grown lukewarm on female suffrage. Working men (who routinely banned women from their clubs) were as prejudiced as the males of other classes, realised the Pankhursts. So in 1903 they had founded the WSPU to fight on the single issue of votes for women, demonstrating peacefully to start with, but resorting to lawbreaking as they got arrested for 'obstruction'. 'Deeds not Words' was their motto, and their deeds became more extreme as feelings escalated.

Emily Davison's personal motto was 'Freedom against tyrants is obedience to God'. In 1909 she had written the words on slips of paper and tied them to rocks that she hurled at a carriage containing David Lloyd George, the Chancellor of the Exchequer – she had been sentenced to one month in prison.

This was one of seven prison terms that Emily served between 1909 and 1912 for offences that included obstruction and breaking windows in the House of Commons. Her longest sentence was six months for setting fire to public postboxes. 'Argument is no use,' she once said, defending the fierceness of suffragette demonstrations, 'writing, speaking, pleading – all no use.'

Going on hunger strike while in prison, Emily suffered the dreadful ordeal of forcible feeding: she was held down while a rubber tube was pushed down her throat or up her nostril, then, inevitably, vomited up the fatty brown soup that was poured down the tube. When she barricaded herself inside her cell to escape the feeding, the authorities flooded it with freezing-cold water. In furious protest, she threw herself down an iron staircase, knocking herself out and seriously damaging her spine. She was never free from pain again.

'I give my life,' she declared, 'as a pledge of my desire that women shall be free.'

So dramatic were some of Emily's protests that history has tended to assume she travelled to Epsom in June 1913 with her mind made up to die. But newsreel film of the incident suggests that she was only trying to slow Anmer down by grabbing his reins – and that was the impression of Jones, the royal jockey. In her pocket were found a return rail ticket, and two flags in the suffragette colours.

'She had concerted a Derby protest without tragedy,' explained Sylvia Pankhurst, Emmeline's second daughter ' – a mere waving of the purple-white-and-green at Tattenham Corner which, by its suddenness, it was hoped, would stop the race.'

Whatever the intentions of Emily Davison, her death did not impress people at the time, only confirming popular prejudice against the wildness of the suffragettes. 'She nearly killed a jockey as well as herself,' complained *The Times*, 'and she brought down a valuable horse . . . Reckless fanaticism is not regarded by [the public] as a qualification for the franchise.'

It took the terrible war of 1914–18 to transform attitudes, as women moved into offices, shops and factories to take over the jobs of men. Mrs Pankhurst suspended suffragette protests – it would be pointless, she argued, to fight for the vote without a country to vote in – and her conciliatory attitude prompted the politicians to climb down.

'Where is the man who would now deny to woman the civil rights she has earned by her hard work?' asked Edwin Montagu, the Minister of Munitions, in 1916. In June 1918, five months before the war ended, the vote was given to women over the age of 30 who were ratepayers (council-tax payers) or married to ratepayers. Ten years later suffrage was extended to all women, on the same terms as men.

In the short term, Emily Davison's gesture on Derby Day may have been counterproductive, but over the years it has come to be romantically symbolic of the fight for women's rights – and that was how her fellow campaigners saw it at the time:

Waiting there in the sun, in that gay scene, among the heedless crowd [wrote the journal *Votes for Women* in June 1913], *she had in her soul the thought, the vision of wronged women. That thought she held to her; that vision she kept before her. Thus inspired, she threw herself into the fierce current of the race. So greatly did she care for freedom that she died for it.*

WHEN CHRISTMAS STOPPED
A WAR

1914

IT STARTED WITH SMALL GLIMMERS OF LIGHT – could they possibly be candles? – flickering on the crusted mud of the enemy trenches a hundred yards or so away. The British sentries could not make them out. At first there were just one or two. Then more appeared, several dozen perhaps – miniature Christmas trees were being hoisted over the parapet, accompanied by strange but unmistakable sounds of jollity. The Germans were singing carols now: *Stille Nacht! Heilige Nacht!* – 'Silent Night, Holy Night'. It was Christmas Eve on the Western Front.

The Christmas trees were presents from the German homeland – tiny conifers shipped in by the thousand to raise morale and, presumably, to encourage their boys to fight more fiercely. But on 24 December 1914 their effect was quite the opposite, for the Germans started to clamber out of their fortified positions. And on the other side of the corpse-littered No Man's Land between the trenches, the British found themselves doing the same.

'I went out, and they shouted "No shooting!" and then somehow the scene became a peaceful one,' wrote Captain R.J. Armes of the 1st Battalion North Staffordshire Regiment in a letter home to his wife. 'All our men got out of their trenches and sat on the parapet. The Germans did the same and they talked to one another in English and broken English. I got on top of the trench and talked German and asked them to sing a German folk song, which they did; then our men sang quite well, and each side clapped and cheered the other.'

'It all happened spontaneously and very mysteriously,' remembered Major Leslie Walkinton, then a seventeen-year-old rifleman. 'A spirit stronger than war was at work that night.'

A bright full moon made for classic Christmas card weather. White frost had crispened and had even brought a certain beauty to the normally glutinous wastes of mud. Captain Armes saw the chance to clear the former turnip field of the dead of both sides, so he negotiated an agreement with his German counterpart. The two officers also agreed 'to have no shooting until midnight tomorrow'.

Similar agreements to celebrate Christmas Day peacefully were being negotiated up and down the war zone around Armentières near Lille in northern France. Elsewhere along the four hundred miles of the Western Front, which stretched from the English Channel to the Swiss border, hostilities continued. But in this little patch of Flanders, a bizarre and rather wonderful interlude was imposing itself upon the lethal squalor of the 'war to end all wars'.

Christmas morning started with burial services, the troops from both sides sometimes lining up together. 'Our padre gave a short sermon, one of the items of which was the 23rd Psalm,' wrote Lance Corporal Alex Imlah of the 6th Battalion Gordon Highlanders. 'Thereafter a German soldier, a divinity student I believe, interpreted the service to the German party. I could not understand what he was saying, but it was beautiful to listen to him because he had such an expressive voice.'

The service over, the two bands of men started fraternising. 'One can hardly believe them capable of the terrible acts that have been laid at their door,' Alex Imlah told his father. 'Some of them could speak English fluently, one of them had been a waiter at the Cecil Hotel, London, and I gathered from them they were pretty well tired of this horrible business.'

The British packages from home included Christmas cards and cigarettes from Buckingham Palace, plus plum puddings from the *Daily Mail*, which formed the basis of some lively barter. Beer, tins of jam, 'Maconochie's' (a canned vegetable stew) and cigars (the Kaiser's Christmas gift to his troops) all changed hands. 'I met a young German officer, and exchanged buttons as souvenirs,' remembered Captain Bruce Bairnsfather of the 1st Battalion Royal Warwickshire Regiment. 'With my wire-cutting pliers I removed a button from his tunic, and gave him one of mine in exchange. Later

I was photographed by a German with several others, in a group composed of both sides.'

In several sectors of the Front the climax of Christmas Day was a series of knock-up football matches, using empty bully-beef cans where balls were not available – one match featured teams of fifty or so per side. Three–two in favour of the Germans was the only result recorded, but the losers did not seem to mind. 'There was not an atom of hate on either side that day,' remembered Bairnsfather.

Such a widespread flowering of peace and friendship had never been seen in the history of war, and it has prompted two myths – that it did not actually happen, or, alternatively, that the truth about 'the Christmas truce' was suppressed by the authorities. Sir John French, the morose commander of the British Expeditionary Force, certainly expressed his 'grave displeasure [at] the reports he has received on recent incidents of unauthorised intercourse with the enemy'. But there was no censorship of the numerous letters in which British officers and men sent home their tales of celebrating Christmas with the enemy, and these were picked up in the newspapers.

These letters also tell the stories of how eventually, and in different ways, the Christmas truce ended. One went like this: 'At 8.30 I fired three shots in the air and put up a flag with "Merry Christmas" on it,' wrote Captain J.C. Dunn of the Royal Welch Fusiliers, whose unit had celebrated with two barrels of beer sent over by the Saxons in the opposite trenches. 'The German captain appeared on the parapet. We both bowed and saluted and got down in our respective trenches, and he fired two shots in the air . . . The War was on again.'

PATRIOTISM IS NOT ENOUGH –
EDITH CAVELL

1915

THE FIRST WORLD WAR STARTED ON 4 AUGUST
1914, when German armies marched into neutral
Belgium, hoping to surprise France and capture Paris. It was
the outcome of a complicated series of international
manoeuvrings that had followed the assassination of
Archduke Franz Ferdinand, heir to the throne of Austria-
Hungary, in Sarajevo, Bosnia-Herzegovina, earlier that
summer. Britain had been trying to stay out of Europe's
quarrels, but she felt impossibly menaced by the prospect of
a German army – and navy – off the English Channel coast.
By the end of August British troops were on their way to
help both the French and the Belgians.

After some early setbacks, the British Expeditionary Force that was sent to France eventually played its part in helping to check the Germans, digging the trenches of what became the Western Front. But the regiments sent to Belgium fared less well. Defeated and outflanked, many British, French and Belgian soldiers found themselves trapped behind enemy lines. If they stayed in uniform they would be captured by the Germans; if they disguised themselves as locals, they risked being shot as spies. Just a few were fortunate enough to find shelter in a nurses' training school on the outskirts of Brussels run by an English matron, Nurse Edith Cavell.

She was a handsome woman, forty-seven years old, with high cheekbones and a luxuriant mass of greying hair that she rolled on top of her head in an elegant chignon. Sharp-eyed and upright, Miss Cavell *looked* like a matron, exuding stern authority. She held a watch in front of her at breakfast, and if any of her nurses arrived more than two minutes late they would be ordered to work an extra two hours. According to one of her staff, she could be 'cold, distant and aloof'.

But matron did not hesitate when Lieutenant Colonel Dudley Boger and Company Sergeant Major Frank Meachin of the 1st Battalion Cheshire Regiment came to her door on a chilly, wet night in November 1914. Boger had a leg wound; he had grown a beard, and was dressed as a Belgian factory worker in a black hat and floppy tie. Meachin was also dressed as a labourer, with rolls of cloth packed between his shoulders to make him look like a hunchback. 'These men are fugitive soldiers,' Cavell told her assistant matron. 'Give them beds in the empty surgical house.'

Boger and Meachin were the first of two hundred such fugitives that Edith Cavell and her staff sheltered at her institute, feeding and tending them until they were strong enough to be on their way. As a young woman Edith had worked as a governess in Brussels for six years, then returned as a nurse in 1907 to pioneer the teaching of Florence Nightingale-style techniques in Belgium. She spoke fluent French and was a respected local figure, trusted by the Belgian underground network: with its assistance, many of her charges were able to find their way home.

'I am helping,' she wrote to her cousin in England, 'in ways I may not describe to you till we are free.'

The Germans announced repeatedly that anyone caught assisting enemy soldiers would be shot, but Edith kept on smuggling fugitives through the hospital. Often she would cook their food at night, serve it herself, then clean up the dishes to get rid of the evidence by dawn. She kept her diary sewn into a footstool.

Unfortunately not all of her fellow conspirators were so careful. One of her contacts in the escape network was arrested, having failed to destroy letters in which Edith's name was mentioned, and on 5 August 1915 the local head of the German secret police arrived at the hospital.

The Germans had no need to torture Edith to discover the truth. She was the daughter of an evangelical Norfolk vicar, and she declined to lie. The only incriminating evidence was a thank you postcard, thoughtfully and thoughtlessly sent by a grateful soldier who had made it home. Tried and found guilty in a single day, Edith's own honest words had effectively condemned her to death. On 12 October she was led out at dawn, blindfolded, and shot by two firing squads, each of eight men, at the national rifle range in Brussels. She was still wearing her nurse's uniform.

The outcry was immediate, both in Britain and around the world – the bitterness provoked by her killing was one of the reasons why there were no more Christmas truces in the trenches. Allied recruitment doubled for eight weeks following her death, and, effectively admitting a tragic error, the Kaiser gave orders that no more women were to be executed without his permission. After the war her body was brought back for a service of thanksgiving in Westminster Abbey, followed by burial at Norwich Cathedral.

Yet Edith Cavell was a war heroine with a difference. On the night before her execution, the English chaplain in Brussels came to offer her consolation, and found instead that the condemned woman had a powerful spiritual insight to offer him: 'Standing, as I do, in view of God and eternity,' she said, 'I realise that patriotism is not enough. I must have no hatred or bitterness towards anyone.'

YOUR COUNTRY NEEDS YOU! –
THE SHEFFIELD PALS

1916

A S THE BRITISH ARMY GATHERED RECRUITS in the summer of 1914, it came up with an attractive offer – men who enlisted together could serve together. Whole neighbourhoods and communities were encouraged to sign up en masse with the promise that they would be able to train and fight together, side by side, as 'pals'.

France, Germany, Austria-Hungary and Russia were raising their armies on the basis of conscription, but Britain's Liberal government balked at making military service compulsory. Volunteers, it was felt, would fight with more spirit than conscripts, and the new War Secretary, Lord Kitchener of Khartoum, was made the focus of a dramatic recruiting campaign.

Horatio Herbert Kitchener was a national war hero who in 1898 had conquered Khartoum – and, indeed, the entire Sudan – then had gone on to secure victory in the Boer War (loyal admirers did not mention his creation of the 'concentration camps'). 'K of K' had striking facial features – fierce, bright eyes and a handlebar moustache of quite extraordinary luxuriance. These figured in a brightly coloured poster in which the great man imperiously pointed directly at the viewer. 'Your Country Needs You!' ran the slogan, and men responded in their tens of thousands. In the 'rush to the colours' of August and September 1914, young friends marched together to the recruiting office, sometimes arm in arm and singing, to enlist in what became known as the pals' (or chums') battalions.*

At full strength a battalion consisted of 1107 officers and men, and in September the Sheffield Pals reached that number in just a few days' recruiting at the Corn Exchange. They were white-collar workers, for the most part – '£500-a-year businessmen,' recalled one recruit, 'stockbrokers, engineers, chemists, metallurgical experts, university and public school men, medical students, journalists, schoolmasters, shop assistants, secretaries, and all sorts of clerks'. 'To Berlin via Corn Exchange' read placards that captured the jingoistic atmosphere of the times.

*More than fifty pals' battalions were formed in 1914/15 from communities all over the country. Among them were the 'bantam' battalions – men who were less than the regulation army height of 5 feet 3 inches (but taller than 5 feet).

Technically known as the 12th (Service) Battalion, York & Lancaster Regiment, the Sheffield Pals started their drill lessons at Bramall Lane, home of Sheffield United Cricket and Football Club. But the stamping of a thousand pairs of boots had a disastrous effect on the turf, and the pals moved on for twelve months of training in various camps, including a spell on Salisbury Plain alongside the 1st and 2nd Barnsley Pals and the Accrington Pals – all grouped together in the 94th Brigade (31st Division).

At the end of 1915, the 31st Division set sail for Egypt to defend the Suez Canal against the threat of a Turkish attack that did not materialise, thereby providing an unexpected holiday in the sun. The office pals from cold northern towns soaked up the late winter warmth of Alexandria – in eighteen months together they had neither lost a life nor fired a shot in anger. But in March 1916 the division was called back to Europe. Britain was preparing a massive assault on the German positions along the River Somme in northeastern France, and the Sheffield Pals had been assigned to capture the village of Serre.

It would be easy, they were told. For a week before their attack, the German positions would be subjected to a non-stop bombardment from the British guns. Nothing would survive – not even a rat – and at the end of June 1916, along the whole length of the Front, one and three-quarter million shells were duly rained down on the enemy. The battalions attacking Serre were instructed to walk steadily across No Man's Land – there was no need to run. Their job would be to occupy and rebuild the vacated German trenches, and they were loaded down with picks, shovels, rolls of wire and mallets accordingly.

At dawn on the morning of 1 July the pals consumed their iron rations, a special bar of chocolate, and a sandwich to give them energy as they went over the top, and at 7.30 a.m., when the British bombardment ceased, they rose to their feet and headed for the German lines – to be met by a devastating hail of bullets. While the pals had been training and travelling for a year, the Germans had been digging – shelving and fortifying their defences to create deep, shell-proof bunkers that they had shored up with concrete and corrugated iron. The British bombardment had claimed very few casualties, and had also made it obvious that an attack was on the way. The machine-gunners were ready.

As the Sheffield Pals moved forward, in four waves, they were mown down by a merciless fusillade. Half of the third and fourth waves did not even make it to No Man's Land. Those who reached the wire struggled vainly to cut it. To their right the Accrington Pals had greater success, actually reaching the German trenches, but they were driven back with horrendous losses – Kitchener's volunteers fell all along the Front. By sunset that day, some twenty thousand British soldiers lay dead along the Somme, with nearly forty thousand wounded – more than half the troops sent into action, and the greatest ever British loss in a single day of battle.*

---

*The Somme offensive continued until 18 November 1916, with the British and the French eventually advancing some 7.5 miles (12 kilometres) – at a cost of some 420,000 British missing, dead or wounded, and a further 200,000 French casualties. German casualties were estimated at 500,000. The village of Serre remained untaken.

The Sheffield Pals had lost more than five hundred, killed, wounded or missing, the pals of Accrington, Barnsley, Bradford, Durham and Leeds falling in similar numbers. They had signed up together, and they perished together – there was scarcely a street in the north of England that did not have a house with its blinds drawn that summer. Two days later the remnants of the Sheffield Pals were taken out of the line: their battalion had virtually ceased to exist.

In the months that followed, their numbers were rebuilt. Conscription was introduced in 1916, and the Sheffield City Battalion would go into battle again at Vimy Ridge in 1917, fighting bravely. But 'pals' they could never be again – not like the original £500-a-year businessmen and 'all sorts of clerks' who had marched to the Corn Exchange so blithely to swap their white collars for khaki.

A COUNTRY FIT FOR HEROES?

1926

EARLY IN NOVEMBER 1920, FOUR MILITARY search parties set off from England to France on a gruesome mission. It was two years since the Great War had ended, and the soldiers were heading for the four principal battlefields, the Aisne, the Somme, Ypres and Arras, with orders to dig up one British body from each. They were instructed to look for badges and scraps of uniform which identified the corpse as belonging to a British regiment, but to exclude bodies with any form of personal identification. The soldier they were looking for must be *unknown*.

Four such unidentifiable British bodies, each covered reverently with a Union Jack, were brought to a chapel in the

Flanders town of St Pol, where an officer – blindfolded, according to some versions of what happened next – indicated which of the four should be placed in a waiting coffin made of oak from Hampton Court. The other three bodies were solemnly reburied, while the Unknown Warrior was taken to Boulogne, then across the English Channel, by warship, to Dover.

Silent crowds – many of them mothers, sisters and widows dressed in mourning – were waiting on the platform of every station through which the train would carry the Warrior from Dover to the capital. 'In the London suburbs,' wrote one reporter, 'there were scores of homes with back doors flung wide, light flooding out, and in the garden figures of men, women and children gazing at the great lighted train rushing past.'

On the morning of 11 November 1920, the anniversary of the Armistice* signed two years earlier, the Unknown Warrior was borne on a gun carriage drawn by six black horses to Westminster Abbey where an honour guard of one hundred VCs was waiting.†

'They buried him among the Kings,' read the text inscribed on his tomb, 'because he had done good toward God and

---

*From the Latin, *armistitium*, literally the arms-stopping, or truce, signed in France on the eleventh hour of the eleventh day of the eleventh month of 1918. This moment is marked today – as it was on 11 November 1920 – by the nationwide observance of two minutes' silence.

†Holders of the Victoria Cross, the supreme award for valour in battle, created after the Crimean War in the name of Queen Victoria (and manufactured from the metal of Russian guns captured at the siege of Sebastopol).

toward his house.'* More than seven hundred thousand young Britons had died in the four years of the Great War, and a further 1.5 million had been wounded – one in ten males had vanished from an entire generation. Now it was the task of those who survived, said the Prime Minister David Lloyd George, 'to make Britain a fit country for heroes to live in'.

Things started off well, with a postwar boom. The old-age pension was doubled and unemployment insurance was extended to just about every worker in the country – here were the dividends of sacrifice. But Britain's once massive share of the world cake was starting to shrink. The USA's powerful intervention at the end of the war had made clear that the UK was no longer 'top nation' – and as manufacturers found their prices undercut by cheaper, better-quality goods from America and Japan, they resorted to the traditional remedies: cutting wages, demanding that their employees work longer hours for the same pay, or throwing them out of work.

In March 1926 a government commission investigating the coal industry recommended a reduction in wages. 'Not a penny off the pay, not a minute on the day,' was the militant response of the miners' union, which inspired the pit owners to their own act of solidarity – a lockout, which denied employment to all miners who were union members. The Trades Union Congress (TUC) promptly called on union

---

*Based on the Old Testament (2 Chronicles 24:16), these words were inscribed by Richard II on the tomb of his treasurer, John Waltham, Bishop of Salisbury, buried in Westminster Abbey.

members across the country to come to the support of the miners, and on 3 May that year Britain found itself in the throes of its first – and, so far, only – General Strike. The empires of Russia, Germany and Austria-Hungary had all been swept away by the social upheaval that marked the final stages of the Great War. Had revolution now come to Britain?

That was certainly the opinion of the gung-ho Chancellor of the Exchequer, Winston Churchill. He called in the army to deliver essential supplies, and also to guard the printing presses, on which he published the *British Gazette*, an aggressive government propaganda sheet. But calmer heads declined to inflame feelings. The recently founded British Broadcasting Company refused to put out official bulletins without presenting the strikers' point of view as well, while King George V used his influence behind the scenes to delay and effectively scuttle a government plan to impound union funds.

'Damned lot of revolutionaries!' exclaimed the pit owner Lord Derby when the King told him he felt sorry for the miners.

'Try living on their wages before you judge them,' was George V's response.

That proved to be the attitude of Britain as a whole. There was widespread sympathy for the miners. But people did not feel that the miner's plight, no matter how dire, justified the entire country being held to ransom. The strike may have been general, but its extent was far from universal. From the start, middle-class opinion lined up solidly behind the government, with university students driving buses and manning lorries to distribute vital supplies. After little more than a week the TUC felt compelled to call off their action, though the miners would defiantly remain out for months.

'Our old country can well be proud of itself,' wrote the King in his diary, 'as during the last nine days there has been a strike in which 4 million people have been affected, not a shot has been fired and no one killed. It shows what a wonderful people we are.'

His Majesty went too far. The General Strike did show that postwar Britain had the sense to hold back from the brink – but a land fit for heroes?

THE GREATEST HISTORY
BOOK EVER

1930

TIMES WERE TOUGH IN THE EARLY 1930s. THE collapse of the American stock market in October 1929 triggered a worldwide economic recession, the Great Depression, which hit Britain hard as a trading nation. By the end of 1930 the value of British exports had fallen by 50 per cent and unemployment had more than doubled to 2.5 million, a fifth of the country's insured workforce.

Walter Sellar and Robert Yeatman were better off than most. Having fought in the Great War (both were wounded – Yeatman was awarded the Military Cross), they met when they studied history together at Oxford. Graduating in 1922, Sellar went to work as a history teacher, while Yeatman entered the developing trade of advertising as a 'copywriter', devising snappy slogans and sales 'copy' for the Kodak camera company.

The two friends kept in touch, amusing each other with the problems they encountered in their very different careers, and Sellar's tales of the elementary mistakes that his pupils made in their history lessons prompted a brilliant idea: why not compile these schoolboy 'howlers' into a new sort of book that would not seek to impress or bewilder readers with its wealth of historical knowledge, but would, rather, amuse and even console them with its humour and its profusion of mistakes?

The result was *1066 and All That*, a slender volume of short paragraphs and humorous drawings that was first published in October 1930, went through eight more editions before the end of that year, and has remained in print ever since. If you have not read it – and even if you have – please turn to its pages as soon as you have finished this book and read the Sellar and Yeatman perspective on Woadicea, the Venomous Bead, Alfred the Cake (who 'ought never to be confused with King Arthur, equally memorable, but probably non-existent'), the Feutile System, Magna Charter and the Pheasants' Revolt, Richard Gare de Lyon, the Burglars of Calais, the Old Suspender and the Young Suspender, Katherine the Arrogant, Anne of Cloves, the Disillusion of the Monasteries, Broody Mary, the Spanish Armadillo, Shakespeare and his rhyming cutlets, the utterly memorable struggle between the Cavaliers (Wrong but Wromantic) and the Roundheads (Right but Repulsive), WilliamanMary, Rotten Burrows, the Industrial Revelation, Florence Nightingown, the Charge of the Fire Brigade, Queen Victoria's Jamboree, the Great War and the Peace to End Peace . . .

Arbitrarily classifying monarchs as 'Good Things' or 'Bad Things', Sellar and Yeatman gently lampooned the prevailing vision of history as an unstoppable progression of brave and clever actions on the way to Britain becoming 'top nation'. Their satire was so gentle at times as to pay affectionate homage to their target, but they sharpened their knives when it came to 'Justifiable Wars': *War against Zulus*. Cause: the Zulus. Zulus Exterminated. Peace with Zulus.'

Their debunking was very much of its time, reflecting the disillusion of the 'lost generation', enticed towards destruction by promises that had proved to be empty. But their bigger point was timeless and brilliant: 'History is not what you thought,' they wrote in their Compulsory Preface (subtitled 'This means You'). '*It is what you can remember.*'

NOT CRICKET – 'BODYLINE'
BOWLING WINS THE ASHES

1933

IT WAS A HOT AUGUST DAY, AND THE SHORT-pitched balls being hurled down the wicket by Yorkshire's W.E. ('Bill') Bowes were bouncing up sharply. They whistled round the ribs – and sometimes round the ears – of Douglas Jardine, Surrey's cool and lofty captain, whose head was protected by nothing more substantial than the patterned cloth of his exclusive Harlequin club cap. In 1932 it was not considered manly for cricketers to wear protective helmets.

'These things lead to reprisals,' complained Pelham 'Plum' Warner, the retired international cricketer-turned-coach, 'and when they begin, goodness knows where they will end.'

But Jardine did not complain. He liked to be challenged, and he had been thinking for some time about this aggressive style of bowling, then known as 'leg theory'. When attacking a right-handed batsman, a fast bowler would set as many as four or five fielders in a semicircle behind the batsman and to his left – the 'leg' side. He would then bowl fast 'bumpers' down the pitch, aimed more or less at the batsman's head and body, which confronted his victim with a difficult choice: he could either duck in an undignified manner, or else brandish his bat wildly in the hope the ball might end up at the boundary. Sometimes it would – but it would also bounce, quite regularly, into the hands of the waiting fielders.

Bowes and Jardine were both international players. They were due to sail that winter to Australia in an attempt to recapture the 'Ashes'* which Australia had won two years earlier, largely thanks to a phenomenal young batsman, Donald Bradman. This neat and businesslike little cricketer had notched up an average of 139 in the Ashes series of 1930 – in the Third Test at Leeds he had scored 334 in a single

---

*Following England's defeat by Australia in 1882, the *Sporting Times* published a mock obituary of English cricket which concluded: 'the body will be cremated and the ashes taken to Australia'. This prompted the burning of a cricket stump whose ashes were placed in an urn and presented to the English team next time it won. Since then the little black urn has been the trophy for which the two countries compete at cricket – though whichever side wins, the urn remains permanently at Lord's Cricket Ground in north London, headquarters of the MCC, the Marylebone Cricket Club, cricket's governing body since 1787. Until 1976 the English cricket team travelled under the name of the MCC who organised the tours.

innings, a world Test batting record – and in 1932–3 it seemed likely he would perform even better on Australia's dusty wickets.

It was clear that England must find some way of neutralising Bradman, and Jardine reckoned that 'leg theory' was the answer. An austere and aloof character, he had been England's captain since 1931, and he knew that he had the bowlers to cause Bradman trouble. Even faster than Bowes were a strapping pair from the coalfields of Nottingham, Harold Larwood and Bill Voce, who could bowl at velocities approaching a hundred miles (160 kilometres) an hour. In the First Test, held at Sydney, Larwood's devastating speed claimed ten wickets, and prompted a local journalist to come up with a new word as he watched the Australian batsmen ducking and diving for their lives. Leg theory? Call it 'bodyline'.

The name stuck. Australia won the Second Test to level the series, but when they went in to bat in the Third Test at Adelaide ten days later, their captain W.M. Woodfull was felled by a ball from Larwood that struck him over the heart. Larwood had not been bowling 'leg theory', but for his next over – to the furious howls of the fifty-thousand-strong crowd – Jardine calmly set a threatening semicircle of 'leg theory' fielders. A shaken Woodfull was dismissed for only 22. Bradman, bowled by Larwood, managed just 8.

That evening the English coach, Plum Warner, went to the Australian dressing-room to enquire after Woodfull's health. 'I don't want to speak to you, Mr Warner,' the angry captain replied. 'There are two teams out there; one is playing cricket, the other is not. It is too great a game to spoil. The matter is in your hands.'

When play resumed after the weekend, the popular little Australian wicket-keeper Bert Oldfield was knocked down by another fierce Larwood bouncer and retired hurt. Larwood had pitched to the offside, bowling to an off-side field, but as far as the Australians were concerned it was 'bodyline'. X-rays revealed a hairline skull fracture.

'In our opinion it is unsportsmanlike,' ran an indignant cable from the Australian Board of Control to the MCC in London. 'Bodyline bowling has assumed such proportions as to menace the best interest of the game.' Whipped up by the press, feelings became so intense as to prompt talks between the governments of Britain and Australia – the harmony of the Empire seemed at stake.

To start with, the MCC backed their captain. They cabled Jardine their congratulations when the Third Test was won (England won the whole series 4–1, cutting Bradman's average down to a relatively fallible 56.57), and they forced the Australians to withdraw the word 'unsportsmanlike'.

But feelings changed, and so did the rules. 'Leg theory' was outlawed – captains could place no more than two fielders where Jardine placed four or five – and when Australia came to play in England in 1934, it was felt that sacrificial victims were required. The MCC requested that Harold Larwood apologise for his bowling in 1932–3, which he stoutly refused to do since he had simply bowled as instructed by his captain. So England's only bowler ever to top the bowling table five times would never play again for his country, while Jardine, aged thirty-three and at the height of his abilities, felt that the time had come to take a diplomatic retirement from Test cricket.

'Bodyline' bowling – hurling, or more usually bouncing the ball at the batsman – still remains a legal tactic in cricket. You may not do it with a 'leg theory' field set behind the batter, nor may you do it too often – law 42 on Fair and Unfair Play sets out the factors that the umpires must consider. But it remains the great divide between the boys' game of cricket and the girls' game of rounders (or baseball, as it is known in the USA): in rounders/baseball the pitcher is penalised if his ball hits the batter, with the statistics recording HBP (hit by pitch).

When, in the summer of 2005, England wanted to win back the Ashes, they turned to Andrew 'Freddie' Flintoff, a dashing batsman and fast bowler who peppered his deliveries with short-pitched balls that shot up fiercely at Australian bodies and heads. It was seventy years after the era of Jardine and Larwood, and the batsmen were now wearing helmets, but 'bodyline' could still get the job done – England won back the Ashes, and the award for player of the series went to Flintoff (24 wickets, 402 runs, 'hits' not recorded).

EDWARD THE ABDICATOR

1936

'THE MORE I THINK OF IT ALL,' WROTE EDWARD, Prince of Wales, shortly after the First World War, 'the more certain I am that . . . the day for Kings & Princes is past, monarchies are out-of-date.' The Prince was touring the Empire to thank countries like Canada and Australia for their help to Britain during the war, but while publicly smiling, he was privately miserable. 'What an unnatural life for a poor little boy of 25,' he wrote after a busy day of shaking hands and posing for photographs. 'I do get so fed up with it & despondent about it sometimes, & begin to feel like "resigning"!!'

Handsome and charming, with a winning smile and a

taste for cocktails and jazz, Edward Prince of Wales was the first young British royal to be a media celebrity. He was cheered and fêted wherever he travelled: his brightly coloured sweaters and his snazzy plus-fours* were copied as the latest fashion statements. But the more famous he grew, the more hollow and valueless he felt. 'How I loathe my job now,' he wrote, 'and this press-"puffed" empty "succès". I feel I'm through with it and long to die.'

The Prince resented the intrusion of the media. 'I can put up with a certain amount of contact with officials and newspapers on official trips,' he explained to one of his staff. 'It's when they get in on my private life that I want to pull out a gun and kill.' He was a young man in pain, the world's first and most spectacular case of celebrity burnout.

The Prince got little sympathy from his gruff father King George V, who had steered the British monarchy through the years of war and revolution that had brought down two European emperors and eight ruling sovereigns. In July 1917 the King renounced his family's German titles and dignities deriving from the House of Hanover and adopted a new, thoroughly British-sounding name, the House of Windsor. At the same time he had reinvented the style of the monarchy, with more emphasis on duty, going out to meet the public and 'setting a good example'. When the Prime Minister, Lloyd George, complained that heavy drinking among munitions workers was hampering the supply of

---

*'Plus-fours' were loose knickerbockers often worn by golfers, deriving their name from the extra four inches (about 10 cm) of cloth required for the overhang at the knee.

ammunition to the Front, the King banned alcohol from royal occasions, offering his guests water, lemonade or ginger beer for three years until the war ended.*

The old King was particularly unhappy at his eldest son's mistresses – a series of glamorous married women with whom the Prince was seen around the nightclubs of London. British newspapers discreetly looked the other way, but the disapproving father prophesied trouble. 'After I am dead,' he said gloomily, 'the boy will ruin himself in twelve months.'

George V died in January 1936, and at first Britain welcomed the modern style of the new King Edward VIII. Unlike his father, who had always refused to fly, Edward liked to travel by aeroplane, and, in another daring departure, would sometimes appear in public without a hat. But in December the Empire learned to its horror that his modern tastes extended to a tough and wise-cracking American girl-friend, Mrs Wallis Warfield Simpson, who had already divorced one husband and was in the process of divorcing Mr Simpson, her second.

Many people liked the fact she was American – the newspapers, who finally broke their silence five weeks after Mrs Simpson appeared in the divorce court, expressed their approval of her nationality. But 'two husbands living' presented an insuperable obstacle to a society that viewed divorce as a moral and social catastrophe. How could a

---

*The King did not enjoy the sacrifice, which was greeted with ribaldry rather than respect, particularly since the announcement of the self-denying edict from Windsor was followed by the words: 'The Earl of Rosebery and the Rt. Hon. A.J. Balfour, M.P., have left the Castle.' Lloyd George himself did not stop serving alcohol in Downing Street.

double divorcee be bowed and curtsied to, or represent Britain to the world? For a start, royal etiquette prohibited divorced or even separated persons from being received at court.

After canvassing his cabinet colleagues and opinion around the Empire, the Prime Minister Stanley Baldwin told the King he would have to choose between his throne and Mrs Simpson – and Edward VIII did not hesitate. Whenever the King talked of Wallis, Baldwin later told his family, his face wore 'such a look of beauty as might have lighted the face of a young knight who had caught a glimpse of the Holy Grail'. On 11 December the King formally abdicated the throne, and gave his reason in a live broadcast to the nation. 'You must believe me when I tell you,' he said in a voice heavy with emotion, 'that I have found it impossible to carry the heavy burden of responsibility and to discharge my duties as King as I would wish to do without the help and support of the woman I love.'

While Edward's supporters seized joyously on the L-word, proclaiming his sacrifice the love story of the century, his critics found the romantic talk vulgar. They blamed Mrs Simpson, the wicked woman who had led the King astray. But if, sixteen years earlier, Edward had been genuine when he talked of 'resigning' from his 'unnatural' and 'out-of-date' job, then Mrs Simpson was not the reason for the abdication. She was the excuse he had finally found – his blessed release from the fearful and empty destiny of being royal.

PEACE FOR OUR TIME! – MR CHAMBERLAIN TAKES A PLANE

1938

NEVILLE CHAMBERLAIN WAS A BIRDWATCHER – he would get up at five in the morning to study the songs of the various species. He knew more Shakespeare than any other British Prime Minister. A lover of music, he inspired the foundation of the Birmingham Symphony Orchestra, while also campaigning to move the city's 'working classes from their hideous and depressing surroundings to cleaner, brighter and more wholesome dwellings'. He was, in short, a thoroughly civilised, decent and well-meaning man. But it was his misfortune to believe that Adolf Hitler could be trusted.

When Chamberlain flew off to Germany to meet Hitler

for the first time, on 15 September 1938, he quoted Hotspur in *Henry IV Part I* – he hoped, he said, to 'pluck from this nettle, danger, this flower, safety'. The danger went back to the Treaty of Versailles that redrew the map of Europe after the First World War, seeking to cut Germany and Austria down to size. Hitler's ambition, it seemed, was to reverse Versailles – the German people, he said, needed living space (*Lebensraum*) – and he had embarked on an unapologetic programme of rearmament and expansion: in 1936 German troops reoccupied the demilitarised Rhineland; in March 1938 they marched into Austria; now, just six months later, they were threatening to occupy Czechoslovakia in order to 'liberate' the three million German-speaking inhabitants of the Sudetenland, that part of the country bordering on Germany.

It was the first time that Chamberlain had ever flown any distance – perhaps it was an expression of his anxiety that he gripped his umbrella tightly as he got on and off the plane. It was also the first example of what would later be known as 'shuttle diplomacy', for he travelled to and from Germany three times between 15 and 30 September, negotiating with Germany, France, Italy and, nominally at least, with Czechoslovakia, in search of a peaceful solution. It was 'horrible, fantastic, incredible', he declared in one broadcast when he got home, that Britain might be drawn into war because 'of a quarrel in a far-away country between people of whom we know nothing'. The Royal Navy was mobilised, gas masks were distributed, and air-raid trenches were dug in Hyde Park.

Britain had no treaty obligation to defend Czechoslovakia.

But France did, and if she was drawn into war with Germany, then Britain would almost certainly need to go to her defence. It was a rerun of 1914 – and less than a quarter of a century later the tragic slaughter of the Great War loomed very large in people's thinking. Britain was not militarily ready for war. More important, she was not psychologically ready to repeat the pain and sacrifice.

When Chamberlain returned from his third trip, this time to a hurriedly convened conference in Munich, he brought the news that people wanted to hear – 'peace with honour. I believe it is peace for our time.' Britain and France had forced Czechoslovakia to hand over the Sudetenland to Germany in return for a pledge of peace from Hitler, who had signed a separate declaration of friendship with Britain. This Anglo-German Declaration, said Chamberlain, was 'symbolic of the desire of our two peoples never to go to war with one another again', and he waved the piece of paper enthusiastically as he stepped down from his plane.

Britain went mad with relief. Frantic crowds massed along the road into London. Chamberlain, said the Scottish socialist James Maxton, had done 'something that the mass of the common people in the world wanted done'. He was received by the new King George VI on the balcony of Buckingham Palace and applauded by every newspaper except the left-wing *Reynolds News*. Downing Street was flooded with umbrellas sent by people expressing their gratitude to the Prime Minister who had brought them peace.

Munich was the fruit of 'appeasement', a foreign policy that successive British governments had been developing since 1931, based on the feeling that the Treaty of Versailles

had saddled several countries – and Germany in particular – with legitimate grievances that threatened the stability
of Europe. Anthony Eden, Foreign Secretary from 1935 to
1938, liked to point out the primary meaning of 'appease' in
the dictionary – 'to bring peace, to settle strife'.

But peace depended on both sides sticking to what they
had promised, and Adolf Hitler considered himself too
clever and powerful for that. Intent on building his Third
Reich,* he wanted the whole of Czechoslovakia – and more.
In March 1939 German troops occupied Prague, then
marched into Poland at the end of the summer.

'Everything I have worked for, everything that I have
hoped for, everything that I have believed in my public life,
has crashed into ruins,' said Chamberlain on 3 September, as
he announced that Britain and Germany were now at war.
When Hitler, following his conquest of Poland, suggested a
European peace conference, Chamberlain rejected the idea
with scorn. No reliance could be placed, he told his sister Ida,
on anything the man said: 'the only chance of peace is the
disappearance of Hitler and that is what we are working for'.

Chamberlain did not head the battle for long. In the
spring of 1940 an Allied attempt to oust German troops
from Norway failed ignominiously, and though it had been
the project of the First Lord of the Admiralty, Winston

---

*Germany's first Reich, or empire, was the Holy Roman Empire, the
confederation of German and central European states that dominated
much of Europe in the Middle Ages. The second was the unified nation
state of Germany that lasted from 1871 to 1918. Hitler's ambition was to
create a *Drittes Reich*, a Third Empire, larger and longer-lived than either.

Churchill, it was the architect of Munich who got the blame. Neville Chamberlain resigned as Prime Minister on 10 May 1940 and died later that year, an object of scorn. Appeasement became a dirty word, with connotations of treachery and cowardice, and the memory of Munich hangs over politics to this day: it was used to justify the British attack on Suez in 1956, and, more recently, the Anglo-American invasion of Iraq.

With hindsight we can see that Chamberlain was mistaken in trusting Hitler – he only postponed the inevitable by a year. But the cheers that greeted his piece of paper in September 1938 suggested he was far from alone in his wishful thinking. And was he really so wrong to try to stop a conflict which, as it turned out, would claim the lives of more than fifty million people?

DUNKIRK – BRITAIN'S ARMY
SAVED BY THE LITTLE BOATS

1940

THE PORT OF DUNKIRK LIES ON THE WIND-
swept northernmost coast of France, surrounded by
gently rolling sand dunes. To the west, just over the horizon,
lies England, and it was in hopes of somehow crossing the
Channel and getting back home that a quarter of a million
defeated British troops (along with some 120,000 French)
came straggling through the grey-green grass at the end of
May 1940.

They had only their rifles and whatever they could carry
on their backs. They had forsaken their tanks and trucks
and field guns. The equipment and supplies of two entire
armies lay scattered behind them across the lowlands of

Belgium – abandoned in panic as the British and French fled for the sea. On 10 May Hitler's troops had launched a massive, rolling onslaught through the Netherlands, Belgium and Luxembourg. The Germans called it *Blitzkrieg*, 'lightning war', and it had smashed open the route to Paris.

By coincidence, 10 May was the day on which, in London, Neville Chamberlain had resigned as Prime Minister, to be succeeded by Winston Churchill. 'I have nothing to offer,' he told the ministers who joined his Cabinet, 'but blood, toil, tears and sweat. We have before us an ordeal of the most grievous kind.' France was lost, and now Hitler had the prospect of taking nearly a quarter of a million British soldiers captive. On the 26th Churchill ordered the navy to head for Dunkirk, with the RAF overhead to give cover.

The problem was how to load the fleeing soldiers off the beaches, since the shallow coastal waters meant that the navy's destroyers and transport vessels had to anchor a quarter of a mile or more offshore. So the call went out to the yacht clubs and seaside resorts of southeast England for the help of a second navy: paddle-steamers and motor-boats, fishing smacks, tugs, yachts, lifeboats and 'All aboard the *Skylark*!' pleasure-boats – just about anything that would float. This oddly assorted flotilla, the 'Armada of the Little Ships', embarked from England on a mercifully calm sea and headed for the beaches of Dunkirk.

Watching from the dunes, a British artillery officer described the scene:

From the margin of the sea, at fairly wide intervals, three long thin black lines protruded into the water, conveying the effect of low wooden breakwaters. These were lines of men, standing in pairs behind one another far out into the water, waiting in queues till boats arrived to transport them, a score or so at a time, to the steamers and warships that were filling up with the last survivors.

Behind them Dunkirk was in flames: 'the whole front was one long continuous line of blazing buildings, a high wall of fire, roaring and darting in tongues of flame, with the smoke pouring upwards'. Above, in the smoke-filled sky, British planes fought it out with the Stuka dive-bombers of the Luftwaffe (the German air force, literally 'air weapon'). 'One bomber that had been particularly offensive,' wrote C. H. Lightoller, a retired naval officer who had sailed his yacht *Sundowner* across the Channel, 'itself came under the notice of one of our fighters, and suddenly plunged vertically into the sea just about fifty yards astern of us. It was the only time any man ever raised his voice above a conversational tone, but as that big black bomber hit the water, they raised an echoing cheer.'

For nine days and nights the evacuation continued round the clock. Churchill had predicted that 30,000 men might be lifted off; Admiral Ramsay, the officer in charge of the rescue, hoped for 45,000. In the event, virtually everyone who made it to the Dunkirk beaches, some 330,000 men – 220,000 British, 110,000 French and Belgian – was miraculously saved.

Churchill was rightly cautious in his relief: 'Wars are not won by evacuations,' he warned the House of Commons. But saving the vast bulk of the professional army provided Britain with the practical means to keep on fighting – and, more vitally, gave the country a new sense of purpose. In certain respects, the story of the little boats was exaggerated: many had sailed for money, a good number were commanded by active naval officers, and it was the 'big ships' of the Royal Navy that transported the vast majority of the soldiers home.

But if it was a myth, it was a necessary and inspiring myth, symbolising how ordinary people could make a difference. In the weeks that followed, over a million men enrolled in the Local Defence Volunteers; roadblocks and concrete pillboxes sprang up all over the countryside; signposts were removed or craftily rearranged to fool invaders; and the coast was wreathed with barbed wire. 'We shall fight on the beaches,' proclaimed Churchill, 'we shall fight on the landing grounds, we shall fight in the fields and in the streets, we shall fight in the hills; we shall never surrender.'

Britain had drifted rather vaguely through the opening months of what had been known as the 'phoney war'. Now she started to believe in herself – and helped others to believe in her too. Previously detached, America removed the restrictions on getting involved in the European conflict: half a million rifles were dispatched to Britain in the first weeks of June 1940, for, as the *New York Times* explained to its readers, the issues at stake had been made clear at Dunkirk:

> *In that harbour, such a hell on earth as never blazed before, at the end of a lost battle, the rags and blemishes that had hidden the soul of democracy fell away. There, beaten but unconquered, she faced the enemy, this shining thing in the souls of free men, which Hitler cannot command. It is in the great tradition of democracy. It is a future. It is victory.*

BATTLE OF BRITAIN –
THE FEW AND THE MANY

1940

WHEN HITLER HEARD IN THE MIDDLE OF June 1940 that the French government was ready to sue for peace, he instructed them to send their negotiators to the town of Compiègne in northern France. This was where Germany's generals had signed the Armistice in November 1918 at the end of the First World War, in a railway carriage that had been triumphantly preserved in the local museum. Hitler had the carriage taken out of the museum and met the French inside it on the 22nd of that month. After they had signed their humiliating surrender, handing over two-thirds of France to German occupation, the Führer (leader) had the railway carriage taken back to

Berlin as his own trophy of war, then ordered that the Armistice site be obliterated.

After Dunkirk, no one could doubt that Hitler was planning some equally gleeful humiliation for London. He ordered his generals to start planning an invasion, code-named *Seelöwe* (sea lion), to be preceded by a massive aerial attack that would wipe out the RAF. The staff of Hermann Goering, commander of the Luftwaffe, reckoned they could deal with RAF Fighter Command in four days or so of pitched battle, then spend four weeks bombing Britain's major cities and munitions factories into oblivion.

On 10 July the Germans put the first stage of their strategy into practice – dive-bombing merchant ships in the English Channel: apart from sinking vital cargoes, their plan was to lure British fighter planes out to give battle. Since the Luftwaffe probably had three times more planes than the RAF, it would be only a matter of time before Britain was defenceless.

Winston Churchill conjured up another of his ringing declamations in tribute to the airmen who took part in the great battle that followed. 'Never in the field of human conflict was so much owed by so many to so few,' he declared on 20 August, and the young heroes of the RAF who were 'scrambling' as many as five times a day into the skies above southern England that summer were certainly 'few' in number – no more than two thousand or so. But every fighter pilot depended on a massive and complex pyramid of support staff – radar technicians, the observer corps, search-light and barrage-balloon operators, chart plotters, telephone operators, telephone engineers, dispatch riders, signallers and runway repair crews, not to mention the mechanics who produced, maintained and repaired the fighter planes that enabled the Few to win their dogfights. The inside story of the Battle of Britain was the triumph of the Many.

This formidably efficient back-up organisation, unparalleled in aerial warfare to that point, was the work of Air Marshal Sir Hugh Dowding, a cagey character generally disliked by his fellow airmen, who nicknamed him 'Stuffy'. In fact, 'Stuffy' had some most original and unstuffy personal interests that included theosophy* and a belief in fairies, angels, flying saucers and the possibility of intelligent communication between the living and the dead. As one of the first pilots in the Royal Flying Corps (which became the RAF) and a squadron commander in the First World War, he had experimented with Marconi's discovery that messages could be transmitted without connecting cables. He claimed to be 'the first person, certainly in England if not the world, to listen to a wireless telephone message from the air', and he had no doubt that technical superiority was the first principle of aerial warfare.

Dowding's second principle was not to risk expensive machines and the lives of trained airmen unnecessarily. So when the Germans started their *Kanalkampf* in July, dive-bombing in the Channel, he refused to be tempted. He sent up a few fighters, but kept his main squadrons in reserve. Earlier that summer he had successfully persuaded Churchill not to send too many precious Spitfires to the hopeless cause

---

*Theosophy was a movement seeking a universal truth common to all religions. Among its adherents was Annie Besant (see pp. 179-182).

of saving France from the Germans. The secret of success in the coming battle for Britain would be to keep planes in the sky.

In this key objective Dowding was aided by another abrasive but effective character, Lord Beaverbrook, the Canadian proprietor of the *Daily Express* whom Churchill brought into his Cabinet in May 1940 as Minister of Aircraft Production. Manufacture was already running smoothly – 163 new Spitfires came out of the factories that August, along with 251 Hurricanes. But in three short months Beaverbrook dramatically stepped up the maintenance and repair of existing aircraft: 35 per cent of all planes issued to pilots in the Battle of Britain were repaired rather than new; 61 per cent of all damaged planes were returned to active service, and the remaining 39 per cent were 'cannibalised' for spare parts.

The Germans could not match this turn-around rate – as they could not match the planes themselves. The Supermarine Spitfire and the Hawker Hurricane were highly manoeuvrable 'eight-gun' fighters (they had four machine-guns mounted in each wing) and they rapidly disposed of the once-feared Stuka dive-bomber. They also proved more than equal to Germany's best fighter, the Messerschmitt 109 that was handicapped by low fuel capacity: if a Messerschmitt got to London it could fight for only ten minutes before having to turn tail and head back to base.

No one realised it at the time, but from mid-August to mid-September, each day of the Battle of Britain saw the RAF lose significantly fewer planes than the Luftwaffe – 832 in total to Germany's 1268. On 17 September Hitler postponed the invasion of Britain, deciding that Russia offered a more attractive target, and at the end of October he effect-ively admitted defeat when he switched from daytime fighter attacks to night-time bombing.

A few days later, on 9 November 1940, Neville Chamberlain died, a victim of bowel cancer that spared him long enough to see the results of a far-sighted policy. As Chancellor of the Exchequer through the rocky years of the early 1930s, Chamberlain had insisted that the bulk of defence spending be allocated to aerial rearmament, and had raised income tax to five shillings (25p) in the £ to pay for it. So behind the famous Few and the anonymous Many, as organised in the complex back-up system devised by 'Stuffy' Dowding, was the unlikely and unwarlike figure of Neville Chamberlain.

CODE-MAKING, CODE-BREAKING – 'THE LIFE THAT I HAVE'

1943

LEO MARKS WAS SOMETHING OF A LONER AT school – he loved to retreat into his own private world of word puzzles and codes. So as Britain fought its intelligence war with Germany, the young code enthusiast was an obvious candidate for Bletchley Park, the mansion 'somewhere in the country' that was the centre of the nation's code-breakers. Bletchley's great coup was its deciphering, early in the war, of the German 'Enigma' encoding machine that gave Britain advance knowledge of enemy war plans.

To his initial disappointment, the 22-year-old was the one member of his induction course who did not move on to

Bletchley. He was sent instead to the London offices of SOE, the Special Operations Executive which organised the resistance movements behind German lines, following Churchill's order to 'set Europe ablaze'. Leo's job was not to break codes, but to create them for the agents that SOE was parachuting behind the enemy lines, and he rapidly rose to become SOE's head of communications. In his few hours off work, he met and fell in love with Ruth, a nurse who was training for air ambulance work – only to lose her in 1943 when she was killed in an air crash.

Distraught with grief, the code-maker went up on to the nearest roof, and as he gazed up at the stars he imagined Ruth among them, mentally transmitting to her a poem:

> *The life that I have*
> *Is all that I have*
> *And the life that I have*
> *Is yours.*
>
> *The love that I have*
> *Of the life that I have*
> *Is yours and yours and yours.*
>
> *A sleep I shall have*
> *A rest I shall have*
> *Yet death will be but a pause.*
>
> *For the peace of my years*
> *In the long green grass*
> *Will be yours and yours and yours.*

A few months later, in the spring of 1944, Leo was organising the codes for Violette Szabo, a young French resistance worker who had been working under cover in German-occupied France, helping to blow up bridges and railway lines to interrupt the Nazis' supply lines. Violette was due to be parachuted back into enemy territory to help prepare the ground for D-Day, the Allied invasion of northern France, but she was having trouble remembering her code. Every secret agent had to memorise a verse whose letters created a code that was unique to them, and Violette kept forgetting hers – until, in desperation, Leo produced the lines that he had written for Ruth.

'I could learn this in a few minutes,' she said, and when Leo tested her next day, her codes were word-perfect. As a token of gratitude, she presented him with the perfect present for a code-master – a miniature chess set.

Later that summer SOE received news that Violette had been ambushed in France and transported to the German labour camp of Ravensbrück. A few weeks later came worse news. After brutal torture by the Gestapo, she had been executed – shot through the back of the head as she knelt, holding hands with two other captured female agents.

After the war, Violette Szabo's life story was made into a film, *Carve Her Name with Pride*, and many thousands of cinema-goers were moved by her code poem 'The Life That I Have'.

'Dear Code-Master,' wrote one eight-year-old boy in his own personally devised code, which Leo had to work hard to decipher. 'She was very brave. Please, how does the poem work? I'm going to be a spy when I grow up.'

A covering letter from the boy's father explained that his son was desperately ill, so Leo sent the invalid a present – Violette's own chess set, with an invitation, when he got better, to come and meet some of her fellow agents. The SOE's master cryptographer composed his reply in the eight-year-old's personal code, and was delighted to hear that his letter had helped the child rally for a month. The miniature chess set and the memorable code poem were at his bedside when he died.

VOICE OF THE PEOPLE

1945

WINSTON CHURCHILL WROTE ALL HIS OWN speeches. He would spend as many as six or eight hours polishing and rehearsing his words to get the impact just right – and it was worth the effort. 'Let us therefore brace ourselves to our duties,' he declaimed in Parliament on 18 June 1940, 'and so bear ourselves that, if the British Empire and its Commonwealth last for a thousand years men will still say, "This was their finest hour."'

He cracked jokes: 'When I warned them [the French government] that Britain would fight on alone whatever they did,' he related at the end of December 1941, 'their generals told their Prime Minister and his divided Cabinet, "in three weeks England will have her neck wrung like a chicken." Some chicken! [Pause] Some neck!'

By the beginning of 1942 Britain had been at war for more than two years and the tide of fortune was starting to change. Three weeks earlier, on 7 December 1941, Japan had bombed the US fleet at anchor in Pearl Harbor on the island of Oahu in Hawaii, bringing America actively on to Britain's side. At the same time the USSR, as a result of Hitler's decision to attack her earlier that year, became an unlikely but extremely powerful ally. 'So we had won after all,' Churchill later wrote in his memoirs. 'We should not be wiped out. Our history would not come to an end.'

Germany and Japan would continue to fight – peace was still nearly four years away. But in 1942 people were already dreaming about the life they wanted when war was over, and their dreams were expressed by the social reformer William Beveridge, who took advantage of a government invitation to inquire into the social services to prepare a report that was effectively a blueprint for a cradle-to-grave 'welfare state'. After the war, proposed Beveridge, a free health service, family allowances, and universal social insurance should produce 'freedom from want by securing to each a minimum income sufficient for subsistence'.

Published in December that year, the Beveridge Report received a cool response from Churchill, but it struck a chord with the war-weary public. Six hundred and thirty-five thousand copies were sold – the best-selling government White Paper in history.*

Churchill would have done well to heed the sales figures. On 8 May 1945 he stood on the balcony of Buckingham Palace alongside King George VI to celebrate VE (Victory in Europe) Day, a solid-gold national hero. Britain had stood up to the tyranny of Hitler's Germany, and the credit for surviving and meeting that challenge was very personally Churchill's: his was the vision and resolution, his were the sweet and inspiring words.

But in the election that followed, the vision and the sweetness abandoned the great orator. 'My friends, I must tell you,' he said in his opening broadcast of the campaign, attacking the plans of the Labour Party, 'that a Socialist policy is abhorrent to the British ideas of freedom.' From statesman to politician again, in one short step. 'Some form of Gestapo,' he claimed, would be needed to enforce the apparatus of state control that went with the Labour Party's plans to take over national resources.

This language horrified those who shared the vision of William Beveridge, but it would take some time to discover the nation's verdict. The votes of British servicemen all over the world had to be gathered and counted, so there was a three-week interlude between polling day on 5 July and the announcement of the result. On the 15th Churchill flew to Potsdam, outside Berlin, for a victory conference with the

---

*'White Papers' set out the proposals of government departments for future policy following a process of consultation and research. Originally they were bound with white covers.

new US President Harry Truman and Joseph Stalin, the leader of Soviet Russia, then flew back to London for the verdict – to discover on the 26th that he had been defeated, and catastrophically. Labour had won power in a landslide victory of 393 seats to 213. The British people wanted change, and after the hardships and sacrifices of war, they liked the sound of the welfare state. Churchill had outlived his usefulness.

The Potsdam Conference was still going on, and was not due to finish until 2 August. So it was the quiet and modest Clement Attlee, leader of the Labour Party and now Prime Minister, who flew out to Berlin to represent Britain in the final discussions. Truman, who was accustomed to American elections at regular, preplanned intervals, and Stalin, who was accustomed to no elections at all, must have been rather confused by Churchill's rapid disappearance and replacement. But that was how democracy had come to work in Britain.

DECODING THE SECRET OF LIFE

1953

YOUNG FRANCIS CRICK WAS ALWAYS ASKING questions. To keep him quiet, his mother gave him a children's encyclopaedia, and it was through reading what the encyclopaedia had to say about galaxies and the hundred trillion cells in the human body, amongst other things, that he decided to become a scientist. It worried him, however, that science had already made so many discoveries. Would there be any left for him?

'Don't you worry,' said his mother. 'When you grow up there will be plenty left for you to discover.'

Crick was twenty-three years old when Britain went to war in 1939. Since he was doing research work in physics, he was co-opted by the Admiralty to help develop magnetic and acoustic mines. Then, with the return to peace, he went to Cambridge, keen to apply the precise techniques of physics and chemistry to the big questions of biology – what is life, for example, and how is it passed on?

'It was generally accepted,' he later recalled, 'that almost every cell has a complete set of instructions located in its genes which determines how the cell grows, metabolizes and functions in relation to other cells. It was also thought that these genes reside on the cell's chromosomes, which were known to consist of both protein and deoxyribonucleic acid [DNA].'

DNA was a mystery to most scientists, but in 1951 Crick met a young American geneticist, James D. Watson, who shared his hunch that DNA was the key to unlocking the identity of living organisms. With his shirt hanging out and his shoelaces often untied, Watson was the archetypal boffin. He arrived in Cambridge with a crew cut, but soon let his hair grow long and straggly so as not to be mistaken for a US airman, of which there were many in East Anglia – after the war they had stayed on at their bases to confront the new threat of Soviet Russia.

Crick and Watson got their break when Maurice Wilkins, a biochemist from King's College, London, showed them the X-ray diffraction image of DNA that he had made with his colleague Rosalind Franklin. This showed a coil, or helix – a key feature of the molecule. Wilkins and Franklin were on the brink of identifying DNA themselves, but they did not work as a team. Franklin felt that Wilkins patronised her, and she retaliated by refusing to show him her work.

Crick and Watson, meanwhile, struck creative sparks off each other in a wild and exploratory working partnership. When one suggested an idea, the other would try to shoot it down, but without malice. They were building huge improvised models of how they imagined the molecule to be, working with brass rods, metal cutouts, drinking straws and plasticine, like children in a preschool playgroup. They would fiddle with the model, argue a bit, have a cup of tea, move the rods some more – until suddenly, on the morning of Saturday 28 February, 1953, hey presto!

'We've discovered the secret of life!' announced Crick as he and Watson walked into The Eagle, an old coaching inn in the middle of Cambridge, where they liked to take lunch. Their breakthrough had been to visualise DNA as a double helix – a winding spiral staircase, each side of which reflected the other. The balustrades were the complementary components of DNA, held together by the rungs, which were hydrogen bonds. If the rungs were broken in two, the ladder could peel apart, with each side becoming the template for a new ladder. So DNA could go on unzipping itself and copying itself indefinitely.

The Englishman and the American announced their discovery in the journal *Nature* that April with more modesty than they had displayed in the public bar of The Eagle. 'It has not escaped our notice,' they wrote in what has been described as the greatest scientific understatement of all time, 'that the specific pairing we have postulated immediately suggests a possible copying mechanism for the genetic material.' In fact, the article had little popular impact. Britain was preoccupied with the forthcoming coronation of the young Queen Elizabeth II, and it was another nine years before Crick and Watson were awarded the Nobel Prize for their discovery, along with Maurice Wilkins (Franklin would have been honoured as well, had she not died of cancer in 1958).

Nowadays everyone is aware of DNA – murderers and rapists are trapped by its evidence, sheep are cloned with its technology, and we worry about the effects of genetic modification on our crops. It is possible for each of us to predict our own personal chances of long life or of obesity, demystifying what used to be matters of providence, fate, or even morality. Religion, philosophy and the law have yet to adapt to this: if we happen to be genetically programmed to eat, procreate or lose our temper to an excessive degree, how can our greed, lust or anger be condemned as sins or crimes? 'It wasn't me, Guv: it was my DNA.'

History itself will have to be rewritten as DNA research changes our perspective on how the motors of human personality and achievement operate. To paraphrase *1066 and All That*, Crick and Watson's extraordinary discovery confronts us with 'the cause of nowadays', and that seems a good point at which to end this particular history book. Indeed, it brings us full circle. In 1997 Oxford University's Institute of Molecular Medicine extracted mitochondrial DNA material from the tooth cavity of Cheddar Man, Britain's oldest complete skeleton, who lived in the caves of the Cheddar Gorge, Somerset, some 7000 years BC and came to a violent end (see *Great Tales*, vol. 1, p. 1). Mitochondrial DNA is inherited unchanged in the maternal line, and having taken swabs from the cheeks of twenty local people, the Oxford scientists

announced that they had found a direct match, a blood relation across nine thousand years and some four hundred
generations – Adrian Targett, aged forty-two, a local history
teacher who lived less than a mile from the caves.
Sometimes the past is closer than we think.

BIBLIOGRAPHY AND
SOURCE NOTES

A truly great British enterprise has recently enriched our reading resources. September 2004 saw the publication of the *Oxford Dictionary of National Biography*, a compilation of 55,557 British lives, male and female, famous and infamous, brave, tragic, comic – and sometimes downright disgraceful. In bound, paper form the *ODNB* comprises sixty volumes. Electronically, it supports a website which offers unrivalled search facilities – you can look up everyone who has the same name as you, for example, the same birthday, or who ever lived in the same locality. It offers you a 'biography' of the day and full-colour illustrations.

You will be lucky if you get it for Christmas. It costs £7500. But most public libraries now stock it or have electronic access to it, so if your local library does not, ask that they do so without delay. Thanks to electronic access, I have been able to rummage in this extraordinary treasure trove, using the reader number on my ticket to my own local library in Westminster. Sitting at home at my computer, at any hour of the day or night, I have been able to check the details of Captain Bligh of the *Bounty*, Thomas Clarkson the slave-trade crusader, Charles Darwin, Florence Nightingale, Mary Seacole, and all the other characters who march through this third and final volume of *Great Tales from English History* – including the mythical ones, Ned Ludd, Captain Swing and the Unknown Warrior.

The previous volumes of *Great Tales* list the excellent general histories of Britain by Peter Ackroyd, Norman Davies, Simon Schama, Roy Strong, Michael Wood and others. For the years since 1690, they are joined by:

Ekwall, Eilert, *The Concise Oxford Dictionary of English Place-Names* (Oxford, Clarendon Press), 1960.
Ferguson, Niall, *Empire: How Britain Made the Modern World* (London, Allen Lane), 2003.
O'Gorman, Frank, *The Long Eighteenth Century: British Political and Social History 1688–1832* (London, Arnold), 1997.

For internet sources in addition to the *ODNB* (www. oxforddnb.com), visit the following:

www.bl.uk
www.fordham.edu/halsall
www.history.ac.uk/ihr/resources/index.html
www.library.rdg.ac.uk/home.html

There are many other history websites, notably the BBC (www.bbc.co.uk/history), Spartacus (www.spartacus.schoolnet.co.uk) and the History Learning site (www.historylearningsite.co.uk), but those listed above specialise in original documents, some in facsimile and usually with translation provided. On any subject it is worth checking to see what the National Archives have to offer: www.nationalarchives.gov.uk.

The History Place (www.historyplace.com/speeches) has a collection of memorable speeches of recent times, from Elizabeth I's Armada speech to Winston Churchill's 'Blood, Sweat and Tears'.

FURTHER READING AND PLACES TO VISIT

Tale of a Whale

For tales of the Thames, of monstrous fish, frosts, vagrants, the Lord of Misrule, tide boats and tilt boats, from Wandsworth to Wapping and beyond, consult this modern facsimile, in three volumes, of a Victorian classic:

Humpherus, Henry, *History of the Origin and Progress of the Company of Watermen and Lightermen of the River Thames with Numerous Historical Notes, 1514–1859* (Wakefield, E.P. Microform), 1981.

1690: John Locke and Toleration

www.oregonstate.edu/instruct/phl302/philosophers/locke.html provides a good timeline of Locke's career and also has links to an online version of his *Essay on Human Understanding*.

Goldie, Mark (ed.), *John Locke, Political Essays* (Cambridge, Cambridge University Press), 1997.
Tully, James H. (ed.), *John Locke: A Letter concerning Toleration* (Indianapolis, Hackett), 1983.

1690: 'Remember the Boyne!' – the Birth of the Orangemen

See www.geocities.com/Athens/2430/map.html for a map of the battle, and www.bcpl.net/~cbladey/battle.html for an eyewitness account. For the Orangemen, see www.orangenet.org.

Lenihan, Padraig, *1690: Battle of the Boyne* (Stroud, Tempus), 2003.

1693: Britannia Rules the Waves – the Triangular Trade

Facsimile pages of Thomas Phillips's voyage in the *Hannibal* provide the illustrations for Dr Steve Murdoch's article about the female John Brown on www.historycooperative.org/journals/whc/1.2/murdoch.html. James Walvin relates the early history of African immigrants in Britain.

Thomas, Hugh, *The Slave Trade: History of the Atlantic Slave Trade 1440–1870* (New York, Simon & Schuster), 1987.
Walvin, James, *Black Ivory: Slavery in the British Empire* (Oxford, Blackwell), 2001.

1701: *Jethro Tull's 'Drill' and the Miner's Friend*

At the start of their career, the pop group Jethro Tull chose a different name every week. They played well enough on the evening for which they happened to have picked out the name of the seed-drill inventor to be invited back – so the name stuck, with its connotations of eccentric inventiveness. www.historyguide.org features an intelligent lecture on the origins of the Industrial Revolution – along with some stimulating answers to the question 'What is history?'

1704: *Marlborough Catches the French Sleeping at the 'Village of the Blind'*

Two recent books tell the story of John Churchill's brilliant victory – then there is the biography of the great man by his famous twentieth-century descendant. To inspect the glories of Blenheim, visit www.blenheimpalace.com.

Chandler, David, *Blenheim Preparation: The English Army on the March to the Danube* (London, Spellmount), 2004.
Churchill, Winston S., *Marlborough, His Life and Times* (London, 4 vols, Harrap), 1933–8.
Spencer, Charles, *Blenheim: Battle for Europe* (London, Weidenfeld & Nicolson), 2004.

1707: *Union Jack*

For details of the Union Jack, and everything you ever wanted to know about vexillology (the scientific study of flags and related emblems), see www.flaginstitute.org.

1714: *Made in Germany*
Plumb's remains the classic account of the early Hanoverian years.

Hatton, Ragnhild, *George I* (Yale, Yale University Press), 2001.
Plumb, J.H., *The First Four Georges* (London, Collins), 1956.

1720: *The South Sea Bubble*
Charles Mackay's *Extraordinary Popular Delusions and the Madness of Crowds* is still useful as the first historical account of the bubble, with good source material and narrative: www.litrix.com/madraven/madne003.htm.

Balen, Malcolm, *A Very English Deceit* (London, Fourth Estate), 2002.

1721–42: *Britain's First Prime Minister*
Jeremy Black has provided the modern updatings of the classic accounts by Jack Plumb.

Black, Jeremy, *Walpole in Power* (Stroud, Tempus), 2001.
Black, Jeremy (ed.), *Britain in the Age of Walpole* (Basingstoke, Palgrave Macmillan), 1984
Plumb, J. H., *Sir Robert Walpole: The Making of a Statesman* and *The King's Minister* (London, Cresset Press), 1956 and 1961.

1738: *Born Again*
For the modern version of John Wesley's preaching to the multitudes, wherever they might be, visit www.methodist.org.uk. Wesley's letters and sermons can be found on a website run by the Wesley Center for Applied Theology at the Northwest Nazarene Christian University in Idaho: http://wesley.nnu.edu.

Hattersley, Roy, *John Wesley: A Brand from the Burning* (London, Little, Brown), 2002.

1739: Dick Turpin – 'Stand and Deliver!'

This account of the myth of Dick Turpin is largely based on the pioneering research and analysis of James Sharp. For additional historical detail consult the irresistibly named www.stand-and-deliver.org.uk.

Sharp, James, *Dick Turpin: The Myth of the English Highwayman* (London, Profile Books), 2004.

1745: God Save the King!

Frank McLynn began an important modern reassessment of Bonnie Prince Charlie. For a Scottish view of the Battle of Culloden – and of many other things – consult the website www.highlanderweb.co.uk.

McLynn, Frank, *Charles Edward Stuart: A Tragedy in Many Acts* (Oxford, Oxford Paperbacks), 1991.

1755: Dr Johnson's Dictionary

There are numerous popular editions of James Boswell's classic *Life of Johnson*, rich in colour and anecdote. If you want to see where the Doctor worked on his dictionary, you can visit his house, just off Fleet Street in London. See www.drjohnsonshouse.org.

Lynch, Jack, *Samuel Johnson's Dictionary: Selections from the 1755 Work That Defined the English Language* (London, Atlantic Books), 2004.

1759: General Wolfe and the Capture of Quebec

Canadian websites do James Wolfe proud. www.uppercanadahistory.ca contains a graphic account of the battle on the Heights of Abraham, and you can view the copy of Gray's *Elegy* given to Wolfe by Katherine Lowther on http://rpo.library.utoronto.ca/poem/882.html.

McLynn, Frank, *1759: The Year Britain Became Master of the World* (London, Jonathan Cape), 2004.

1766: *James Hargreaves and the Spinning Jenny*

Ironbridge Museum in Shropshire is a shrine to the wonders of the Industrial Revolution: www.ironbridge.org.uk. Two excellent websites on the cotton industry are www.cottontimes.co.uk and www.spinningtheweb.org.uk. These provide links with many places to visit in Derbyshire and Lancashire, including the Lewis Museum of Textile Machinery and Sir Richard Arkwright's Masson Mills Working Textile Museum, www.massonmills.co.uk.

1770: *Captain Cook – Master of the Pilotage*

The Captain Cook Memorial Museum is yet another reason for visiting the Yorkshire port of Whitby: www.cookmuseumwhitby. co.uk. Click on www.winthrop.dk/jcook.html and you will be greeted by a stirring rendition of 'Rule Britannia', along with links to books and portraits of Captain Cook, a chronology and family tree, and provocative thoughts on Cook's promise to go 'farther than any other man has been before me . . . as far as I think it possible for a man to go'.

1773: *The Boston Tea Party*

Stanley Weintraub provides a fresh look at the American War of Independence, questioning the assumption that all justice resided with the rebels. John Steele Gordon takes the story forward to explain how the USA, which occupies 6 per cent of the world's landmass and has 6 per cent of its people, has come to account for nearly one third of the world's gross domestic product.

Gordon, John Steele, *An Empire of Wealth* (New York, HarperCollins), 2004.

Weintraub, Stanley, *Iron Tears: America's Battle for Freedom, Britain's Quagmire, 1775–1783* (New York, Simon & Schuster), 2005.

1785: *Thomas Clarkson – the Giant with One Idea*

Adam Hochschild describes how Thomas Clarkson ignited the anti-slavery movement and helped choose William Wilberforce as its figurehead. Wilberforce's abolition speech in the House of Commons on 12 May 1789 drew heavily on Clarkson's research into the horrors of the 'Middle Passage' and can be read at www.brycchancarey.com/abolition/wilberforce2.htm.

Hochschild, Adam, *Bury the Chains: The First International Human Rights Movement* (London, Macmillan), 2005.

1788: *The Madness of King George III*

Of the many biographies, Christopher Hibbert has written the most amiable. Alan Bennett's play and film *The Madness of King George* is the work of a serious history student, based closely on such contemporary sources as Fanny Burney. You can see the superb library that the King created between 1760 and 1820, stacked shelf on shelf in a crystal tower in the lobby of the modern British Library in London – the last place that the King, mad or sane, would have wanted it to be.

Hibbert, Christopher, *George III: A Personal History* (London, Penguin), 1999.
Lacey, Robert, 'The library of George III: collecting for Crown or nation?', *The Court Historian*, vol. 10, 2 (Dec. 2005), pp. 137–47, ISSN 1462–9712.

1789: *'Breadfruit Bligh' and the Mutiny on the* Bounty

Visiting William Bligh's grave in Lambeth, just across the river from the Houses of Parliament, provides a double bonus, since the Church of St Mary-at-Lambeth also houses the Museum of Garden History: www.museumgardenhistory.org. The Pitcairn Islands Study Center contains one of the world's largest collections of historical material relating to the mutiny on the Bounty – www.lareau.org/bounty.html, with further links on http://library.puc.edu/pitcairn.html.

1791: *Thomas Paine and the Rights of Man*

Every year on the nearest Saturday to 8 June, the day of his death, members of the Thomas Paine Society gather at the statue of Paine in Thetford, Norfolk, his birthplace: www.thomaspainesociety.org. The Society also organises lectures by modern radical thinkers, from Germaine Greer to Tony Benn, in the Paine tradition. www.thomaspaine.org is the exhaustive website of the Thomas Paine National Historical Association in America.

1792: *Mary Wollstonecraft and the Rights of Woman*

You can read the text of *A Vindication of the Rights of Woman* on www.bartleby.com/144 and also on www.orst.edu/instruct/phl302/philosophers/wollstonecraft.html.

Todd, Janet, *Mary Wollstonecraft: A Revolutionary Life* (London, Weidenfeld & Nicolson), 2000.

Tomalin, Claire, *The Life and Death of Mary Wollstonecraft* (London, Penguin), 1992.

1805: *England Expects . . .*

The recent bicentennial of the Battle of Trafalgar stimulated a flood of books about Nelson. Janet MacDonald shows how a navy marches on its stomach.

Coleman, Terry, *Nelson: The Man and the Legend* (London, Bloomsbury), 2002.

MacDonald, Janet, *Feeding Nelson's Navy: The True Story of Food at Sea in the Georgian Era* (London, Chatham Publishing), 2004.

1811: *Fanny Burney's Breast*

You can read the text of Fanny Burney's novel *Evelina*, an eighteenth-century *Bridget Jones's Diary* written in letter form, on http://digital.library.upenn.edu/women/burney/evelina/evelina.html. The harrowing tale of her breast removal can be read in Nigel Nicolson's brilliant little book.

Nicolson, Nigel, *Fanny Burney, Mother of English Fiction* (London, Short Books), 2002.

1812: Who Was Ned Ludd?

Ned Ludd may not have existed, but he has earned an entry in the *Oxford Dictionary of National Biography*, along with Robin Hood, King Arthur and his near-contemporary, Captain Swing. The National Archives Learning Curve presents five striking contemporary documents, including a handbill inciting weavers to revolt and one offering a £200 reward to catch men who wrecked machines: www.learningcurve.gov.uk/politics/g3. Thompson remains the classic account of early labour movements.

Thompson, E.P., *The Making of the English Working Class* (London, Gollancz), 1963.

1815: Wellington and Waterloo

English Heritage now takes care of 'Number One, London', Wellington's home at Apsley House at Hyde Park Corner: www.english-heritage.org.uk/server/show/ConProperty.410. Fletcher, Howarth and Keegan analyse the battle from different viewpoints. Hibbert's intimate biography of the 'Iron Duke' is a classic.

Fletcher, Ian, *A Desperate Business: Wellington, the British Army and the Waterloo Campaign* (London, Spellmount), 2001.

Hibbert, Christopher, *Wellington: A Personal History* (London, HarperCollins), 1998.

Howarth, David, *Waterloo: A Near-Run Thing* (Gloucestershire, Windrush Press), 1997.

Keegan, John, *The Face of Battle: A Study of Agincourt, Waterloo and the Somme* (London, Pimlico), 2004.

1823: Stone Treasures – Mary Anning and the Terror Lizards

Every year the Philpott Museum at Lyme Regis is the focus of a festival celebrating Mary Anning and her pioneering of England's

Jurassic coast: www.lymeregismuseum.co.uk/fossils.htm. Dr Hugh Torrens, the geological expert on Mary's life and work, is currently searching for two ichthyosaur fossils whose current whereabouts are unknown. He suspects they are probably sitting in a museum or someone's personal collection gathering dust, so if you think you know their location, please contact Dr Torrens at gga10@keele.ac.uk.

Cadbury, Deborah, *The Dinosaur Hunters* (London, Fourth Estate), 2000.

Freeman, Michael, *Victorians and the Prehistoric: Tracks to a Lost World* (New Haven, Yale University Press), 2004.

McGowan, Christopher, *The Dragon Seekers* (New York, Perseus), 2001.

1830: Blood on the Tracks

This account of William Huskisson's death is largely based on Simon Garfield's recent book, which sheds revealing light on the politician's early career. Rail lovers will already know that the Mecca and Medina of locomotive collections are close to each other in Yorkshire at the Darlington Railway Centre and Museum (www.drcm.org.uk), which offers a virtual tour, and at the National Railway Museum at York (www.nrm.org.uk).

Garfield, Simon, *The Last Journey of William Huskisson* (London, Faber), 2003.

1819–32: The Lung Power of Orator Hunt

Edward Pearce, the modern parliamentary reporter, paints an insightful sketch of Orator Hunt in his historical account of Reform. The Act itself can be viewed at the National Archives website: www.nationalarchives.gov.uk/pathways/citizenship/struggle_democracy/getting_vote.htm.

Pearce, Edward, *Reform! The Fight for the 1832 Reform Act* (London, Jonathan Cape), 2003.

1834: The Tolpuddle Martyrs

The modern cult of the martyrs owes much to the centenary organised by the Trades Union Congress in 1934. Annual rallies have been held ever since in Tolpuddle, where there is a museum and a row of six cottages for retired agricultural workers, each one bearing the name of one of the martyrs: www.tolpuddlemartyrs.org.uk.

Trades Union Congress, *The Book of the Martyrs of Tolpuddle, 1834–1934* (London, TUC), 1934.

1837: 'I Will Be Good' – Victoria Becomes Queen

The world's libraries are overloaded with chunky biographies of Queen Victoria, but the best two studies are the perceptive little volumes by Walter Arnstein and Lady Longford, each of them the distillation of a lifetime's study and thought. Lynne Vallone had a lucky break when she stumbled on boxes in the Royal Archives containing the earnest young Victoria's exercise books, notes on her behaviour during lessons, and some stray bits of blotting paper with little sketches on them – plus a lovely watercolour map that she reprinted in *Becoming Victoria*.

Arnstein, Walter, *Queen Victoria* (Basingstoke, Palgrave Macmillan), 2004.
Longford, Lady Elizabeth, *Queen Victoria* (Pocket Biography Series) (London, Sutton Publishing), 2000.
Vallone, Lynne, *Becoming Victoria* (New Haven, Yale University Press), 2001.

1843: 'God's Wonderful Railway' – Isambard Kingdom Brunel

Depending on where you live, you can experience the soaring vision of Brunel by visiting Paddington or Bristol Temple Meads railway stations, the Clifton Suspension Bridge, or the Royal Albert Bridge crossing the Tamar at Saltash, near Plymouth. You can also tread the deck of the *Great Britain*, now at rest near the replica of John Cabot's *Matthew* in the floating docks at Bristol (another of IKB's achievements).

Brindle, Steve, *Brunel: The Man Who Built the World* (London, Weidenfeld & Nicolson), 2005.

Fox, Stephen, *The Ocean Railway* (London, HarperCollins), 2003.

Griffiths, Denis, with Andrew Lambert and Fred Walker, *Brunel's Ships* (London, Chatham Publishing), 1999.

1843: *Rain, Steam & Speed – the Shimmering Vision of J.M.W. Turner*

When he died in 1851, Turner bequeathed to the nation all his paintings, which he described as 'his children', along with his brushes, paint-smeared palettes and a myriad of his busy, often rain- and spray-spattered notebooks. You can see these on display in a sequence of wonderful rooms at the Tate Britain gallery in Pimlico, London: www.tate.org.uk. But you will have to go to the National Gallery in Trafalgar Square to see *Rain, Steam & Speed*. John Ruskin reproduced the details of Jane O'Meara's memorable train journey with Turner in volume 35 (p. 600) of his collected works.

Ruskin, John, *Works* (London, George Allen), 1908.

1851: *Prince Albert's Crystal Palace*

Michael Leapman's is the latest book to capture the magic of Prince Albert's Great Exhibition, whose splendours are commemorated on a number of websites:

www.victorianstation.com/palace.html
www.bbc.co.uk/history/historic_figures/albert_prince.shtml

Leapman, Michael, *The World for a Shilling* (London, Headline), 2001.

1852: 'Women and Children First!' – the Birkenhead Drill

The *Boy's Own Paper* for 1 November 1884 contains the classic account of the *Birkenhead's* sinking. The estimable Wikipedia project is not always reliable, but this link does contain the list of all those who perished – together with details of the unproved rumour that the *Birkenhead* went down with three tons of gold coins secretly stored in the powder room: http:// en.wikipedia.org/wiki/HMS_Birkenhead

1854: Into the Valley of Death

Cecil Woodham-Smith wrote the classic account of this misadventure. Terry Brighton has presented a modern reassessment. Philip Knightley's ground-breaking book recounts the career of William Howard Russell, along with the history of 'the war correspondent as hero, propagandist and myth maker from the Crimea to Vietnam'. The first casualty of war is, of course, the truth.

Brighton, Terry, *Hell Riders: The True Story of the Charge of the Light Brigade* (London, Henry Holt), 2004.
Knightley, Philip, *The First Casualty* (London, André Deutsch), 1975.
Woodham-Smith, Cecil, *The Reason Why* (London, McGraw-Hill), 1953.

1854–5: The Lady of the Lamp and the Lady with the Teacup (plus the Odd Sip of Brandy)

Just across the Thames from the Houses of Parliament, the Florence Nightingale Museum in St Thomas's Hospital contains, among other memorabilia, Florence Nightingale's pet owl, Athena, stuffed and preserved in a glass case: www.florence-nightingale.co.uk. Thames Valley University hosts a handsome website www.maryseacole.com, and the Department of Health offers annual leadership awards up to £12,500 for black and minority ethnic nurses, midwives and health visitors in the NHS in honour of Mary Seacole: www.nhsemployers.org/excellence/excellence-692.cfm.

Salih, Sara (ed.), *Wonderful Adventures of Mrs Seacole in Many Lands* (London, Penguin), 2005.

Woodham-Smith, Cecil, *Florence Nightingale, 1820–1910* (London, Fontana), 1969.

1858: Charles Darwin and the Survival of the Fittest

You could spend your whole life reading books about Darwin – and another lifetime studying the work of Alfred Russel Wallace (the spelling of whose middle name was perpetuated from a mistake made when his birth was recorded).

Browne, Janet, *Charles Darwin* (New York, Knopf), 2002.

Slotten, Ross A., *The Heretic in Darwin's Court: The Life of Alfred Russel Wallace* (New York, Columbia University Press), 2004.

1878: The Great Stink – and the Tragedy of the Princess Alice

This account is largely based on Jonathan Schneer's evocative history of the Thames, as entrancing and meandering as the river itself. For more on the remarkable architect of London's sewers, go to www.bbc.co.uk/history, and search for Joseph Bazalgette.

Schneer, Jonathan, *The Thames: England's River* (London, Little, Brown), 2005.

1887: Lord Rosebery's Historical Howler

The file copy of Queen Victoria's letter to Lord Rosebery is in the Royal Archives at Windsor, RA/VIC/F47/49, reproduced by gracious permission of Her Majesty the Queen. The original is in the Rosebery Archive at the National Library of Scotland, MS10064, ff 114-17.

Rhodes James, Robert, *Rosebery* (London, Weidenfeld & Nicolson), 1963.

1888: Annie Besant and 'Phossy Jaw' – the Strike of the Match Girls

Annie's philosophical journey from minister's wife to atheist to theosophist is well described in http://womenshistory. about.com/od/freethought/aannie_besant.htm. For the horrors of phossy jaw, visit http://en.wikipedia.org/wiki/Phossy-jaw.

1897: Diamond Jubilee – the Empire Marches By

Kuhn's seminal work describes the transformation of the British monarchy in the latter part of Queen Victoria's reign. Hudson illuminates the thinking and preparation behind the two great royal festivals.

Hudson, Roger, *The Jubilee Years 1887–1897* (London, Folio Society), 1996.

Kuhn, William, *Democratic Royalism: The Transformation of the British Monarchy 1861–1914* (London, Macmillan), 1996.

1900: Slaughter on Spion Kop

From the 1902 account by Arthur Conan Doyle (creator of Sherlock Holmes), the Boer War has been well served by lively authors, of which Thomas Pakenham is the finest. www.anglo-boer.co.za/index.html offers a 'virtual museum' of Boer War history to stroll through.

Pakenham, Thomas, *The Boer War* (London, Folio Society), 1999.

1903: Edward VII and the Entente Cordiale

Oxford's Bodleian Library gathered some unusual news clippings to mark the centenary of the Entente Cordiale, which can be reached via www.bodley.ox.ac.uk, then searching for Entente Cordiale. If you would like to win an £8000 post-graduate scholarship to study in Paris, go to www.entente-cordiale.org.

Dunlop, Ian, *Edward VII and the Entente Cordiale* (London, Constable), 2004.

Heffer, Simon, *Power and Place: The Political Consequences of King Edward VII* (London, Weidenfeld & Nicolson), 1998.

1910: *Cellar Murderer Caught by Wireless – Dr Crippen*
The Metropolitan Police website gives major coverage to one of its most famous cases, and while you are visiting www.met.police.uk/history, why not sample more stories from the Crime Museum – Jack the Ripper, the Brides in the Bath murders, and the dreadful doings of the Kray twins?

Smith, David James, *Supper with the Crippens: A New Investigation into One of the Most Notorious Cases of the Twentieth Century* (London, Orion), 2005.

1912: *'I May Be Some Time . . .' – the Sacrifice of Captain Oates*
The Scott Polar Research Institute – www.spri.cam.ac.uk – just around the corner from the Fitzwilliam Museum in Cambridge, has Captain Oates's reindeer-skin sleeping bag on display. The archives are rich with the letters and diaries of Polar explorers (north and south) – though Scott's diary of his last expedition is at the British Museum in London.

Limb, Sue, and Patrick Cordingley, *Captain Oates, Soldier and Explorer* (London, Batsford), 1982.
Scott, R. F., *Scott's Last Expedition: The Journals of Captain R. F. Scott* (London, Pan), 2003.

1913: *The King's Horse and Emily Davison*
The admirable Spartacus website shows a photograph of Emily Davison at her graduation, along with extracts from contemporary newspapers and memoirs: www.spartacus.schoolnet.co.uk/Wdavison.htm. For more on the suffragette movement, visit www.historylearningsite.co.uk/women%201900_1945.htm, as well as the history website of the BBC, www.bbc.co.uk/history, which has a rich archive on women's movements in Britain and abroad.

1914: *When Christmas Stopped a War*

www.firstworldwar.com is an encyclopaedic survey of the Great War, month by month, reproducing propaganda posters, memoirs, diaries and primary documents of all sorts, together with contemporary photographs and battlefield maps. Bruce Bairnsfather became the cartoonist of trench warfare, creating the character 'Old Bill'.

Marsay, Mark (ed.), *The Bairnsfather Omnibus: 'Bullets and Billets' and 'From Mud to Mufti'* (Scarborough, Great Northern Publishing), 2000.

Weintraub, Stanley, *Silent Night: The Remarkable Christmas Truce of 1914* (London, Simon & Schuster), 2001.

1915: *Patriotism Is Not Enough – Edith Cavell*

'Humanity, Fortitude, Devotion, Sacrifice' is the inscription on the tall stone memorial to Edith Cavell which offers an inspiring sight outside the National Portrait Gallery, just off Trafalgar Square in London. The Edith Cavell website is a lovingly tended garden of tributes and memorabilia including photographs of the Norfolk rectory where she grew up, and the interior of the cell in which she spent her final hours: www.edithcavell.org.uk.

1916: *Your Country Needs You! – the Sheffield Pals*

www.firstworldwar.com contains detailed entries on the Pals' regiments and also on the ghastly battles of the Somme offensive. Extracts from Richard Sparling's detailed history of the Sheffield Pals can be found on their website, www.pals.org.uk/sheffield.

Sparling, Richard, *History of the 12th (Service) Battalion, York and Lancaster Regiment* (Sheffield, J.W. Northend), 1920.

1926: *A Country Fit for Heroes?*

www.aftermathww1.com dates itself from Armistice Day, 31,909 days ago by the end of March 2006. The purpose of the site is to recall what happened 'when the boys came home'. Kenneth Rose's prize-winning biography recounts the drama of the General Strike as seen from Buckingham Palace.

Rose, Kenneth, *George V* (London, Phoenix), 2000.

1930: *The Greatest History Book Ever*
'Histories have previously been written with the object of exalting their authors. The object of this History is to console the reader. *No other history does this.*'

Sellar, W. C., and R. J. Yeatman, *1066 and All That* (London, Methuen), 1930.

1933: *Not Cricket – 'Bodyline' Bowling Wins the Ashes*
www.cricinfo.com will connect you with the *Wisden Cricketers' Almanack*, the bible of the game. www.lords.org is the detailed and helpful website of the MCC, which will tell you how to visit the museum at Lord's, where you can see the little urn containing the Ashes. For detailed score sheets of every Test Match in the bodyline series, see www.334notout.com.

Frith, David, *Bodyline Autopsy: The Full Story of the Most Sensational Test Cricket Series – England vs. Australia 1932–3* (London, Aurum Press), 2003.

1936: *Edward the Abdicator*
Edward VIII's abdication speech can be read in full on www.historyplace.com/speeches/edward.htm. Philip Ziegler wrote the official and definitive biography (not always the same thing). Rupert Godfrey edited the letters in which the young Prince of Wales expressed his despair at his royal lot.

Godfrey, Rupert (ed.), *Letters from a Prince: Edward Prince of Wales to Mrs Freda Dudley Ward, March 1918–January 1921* (London, Time Warner Books), 1999.
Ziegler, Philip, *Edward VIII* (London, HarperCollins), 1990.

1938: Peace for Our Time! – Mr Chamberlain Takes a Plane

Keith Robbins brilliantly captures the touch-and-go atmosphere of 1938 in his comprehensive study. Parker shows how 'appeasement' should mean much more to us than another word for 'caving in'.

Parker, R.A.C., *Chamberlain and Appeasement* (London, Macmillan), 1993.
Robbins, Keith, *Munich* (London, Cassell), 1968.

1940: Dunkirk – Britain's Army Saved by the Little Boats

The Association of Dunkirk Little Ships commemorates the heroes who crossed the Channel and gives details of surviving boats when they come up for sale: www.adls.org.uk.

Wilson, Patrick, *Dunkirk* (Barnsley, Pen & Sword Books), 1999.

1940: Battle of Britain – the Few and the Many

www.battleofbritain.net and www.the-battle-of-britain.co.uk provide detailed lists of the combatants on both sides. Among them was Joseph Frantisek of the Polish Air Force, with 17 confirmed kills. He flew with 303 Squadron (named after the Polish hero, General Tadeusz Kosciuszko), which claimed to have downed 126 enemy planes, the highest number achieved by any fighter squadron engaged in the Battle of Britain.

Craig, Phil, and Tim Clayton, *Finest Hour* (London, Hodder & Stoughton), 1999.
Olsen, Lynne, and Stanley Cloud, *A Question of Honor: The Kosciuszko Squadron: Forgotten Heroes of World War II* (New York, Knopf), 2003.

1943: Code-making, Code-breaking – 'The Life That I Have'

Like Leo Marks, Alan Turing was an unconventional character whose creativity made an immense contribution to the secret war effort – working at Bletchley Park, he cracked the secret of the

Enigma code. His intriguing and ultimately tragic story can be read on www.turing.org.uk. The official story is recounted on www.bletchleypark.org.uk, which tells you how you can visit Bletchley Park near Milton Keynes in Buckinghamshire.

Marks, Leo, *Between Silk and Cyanide: A Code-Maker's Story, 1941–1945* (London, HarperCollins), 1998.
Montefiore, Hugh Sebag, *Enigma: The Battle for the Code* (London, Weidenfeld & Nicolson), 2000.

1945: *Voice of the People*
You can hear Winston Churchill speak when you click on the website of the Churchill Society. www.churchill-society-london.org.uk also includes the text of his famous 'Iron Curtain' speech delivered at Fulton, Missouri, in 1946.

Harris, Jose, *William Beveridge: A Biography* (Oxford, Clarendon Press), 1997.
Reynolds, David, *In Command of History: Churchill Fighting and Writing the Second World War* (London, Longman), 1992.

1953: *Decoding the Secret of Life*
The finest account of DNA's decoding is James D. Watson's own engaging memoir on the search for the double helix. Before his death, Francis Crick recounted his side of the story in a long interview which can be read on www.accessexcellence.org, along with other articles about the pair. Brenda Maddox's award-winning book documents the tale of the 'Dark Lady' of DNA.

Maddox, Brenda, *Rosalind Franklin* (London, HarperCollins), 2003.
Watson, James D., *The Double Helix: A Personal Account of the Discovery of the Structure of DNA* (London, Penguin), 1999.

ACKNOWLEDGEMENTS

The earlier volumes of *Great Tales* have prompted a host of friendly letters from readers, some of whom have suggested stories that appear in this book. Phil Turton proposed the 'bodyline' tour as a modern morality tale; Clive Fairweather, whose vocation is the telling of traditional stories, passed on the vivid tableau of J.M.W. Turner sticking his head out of the railway carriage window, together with another even more dark and stormy episode, the sinking of the *Birkenhead*.

I am most grateful to the professional historians who have provided me with help and advice, headed by my friend from Bristol Grammar School, Professor Keith Robbins, and Dr Jonathan Conlin, whom I came to know through our mutual devotion to *1066 and All That*. Professor Walter Arnstein, Professor Lynne Vallone and Dr Yvonne Ward gave me particular guidance on matters Victorian. From Cheddar Man onwards, Professor Alfred Smyth has been a generous counsellor – his Anglo-Saxon knowledge was a particular help when it came to the meaning of Tolpuddle – and my thanks also go to his wife Margaret. My coverage of the Crimean War owes much to Professor Elizabeth Anionwu of the

Mary Seacole Centre for Nursing Practice, Thames Valley University.

I am grateful to the librarians of the National Archives, the British Library, the London Library and the Westminster Public Library, as well as to the partners of the John Sandoe Bookshop. Christopher Skidmore has provided invaluable guidance with my background reading for all three volumes, and for the years since 1832 I have received the newspaper and magazine research assistance of Charles Donovan.

At the Royal Archives in Windsor, I am most grateful for the help and patience of Pam Clark and Julie Snelling in pursuing the details of Lord Rosebery's historical howler. Christopher Lloyd has helped me track down possible pictorial evidence for the tale, with the assistance of Vanessa Remington; Sheila Mackenzie at the National Library of Scotland gave help with the Rosebery Archive. My thanks to Matthew Engel of *Wisden* for his masterly exposition of 'leg theory', and to Glenys Williams, Archivist of the MCC at Lord's.

The visual style of all three volumes has been set by the evocative and quizzical illustrations of Fred van Deelen – it has been such a pleasure to have his illustrations zipping over the broadband with the dawn. My thanks to Moyra Ashford, who got me as far as Captain Bligh and Mary Wollstonecraft, and to my dear wife Sandi. Christine Todd has actually made the preparation of the Bibliography and source notes seem like fun.

This third volume is dedicated to the youngest of my children, Bruno, who provided critical comments on the earlier *Tales* and brought his anthropological expertise to bear on this volume by tracking down learned articles on the dismemberment of Captain Cook.

At Little, Brown, my mentors Roger Cazalet and Viv Redman have encouraged, supported and challenged me marvellously. My thanks to Peter Cotton for yet another glorious cover, and to Sue Phillpott for her meticulous copyediting. The book's indexer was David Atkinson and the proofreaders Jane Birkett and Caroline Hogg. Jonathan Pegg and Shaheeda Sabir have backed me up unfailingly at Curtis Brown.

This volume took an extra year to produce as my life changed in some quite dramatic ways. My thanks to Myrto Cutler, Prentis Hancock and Gregorio Kohon who helped keep things clear and bright – and to Jane Rayne, my clearest and brightest new friend.

Robert Lacey, March 2006

INDEX

R OBERT LACEY BEGAN HIS WRITING CAREER
with acclaimed biographies of the Elizabethan heroes
Robert, Earl of Essex, and Sir Walter Ralegh while he was
working as a journalist and assistant editor on the *Sunday
Times* Magazine. With the success of *Majesty*, his Silver
Jubilee biography of Queen Elizabeth II in 1997, he became
a full-time writer, producing a string of bestsellers: *The
Kingdom: Arabia and the House of Saud; Ford: The Man and
the Machine; Sotheby's: Bidding for Class*, and his co-authored
history classic *The Year 1000*. Robert Lacey lives in London.